"A charming narrative . . . the m[...] can't reproduce these dishes exa[...] food can undoubtedly come clos[...] the author on a trip through the[...] appeared as if they were picked [...] day, the fish counter, with innumerable varieties unknown to our American shopper, so fresh 'you'd swear you could see some of the fish still moving'; the meat counter, with everything cut to order; and the cheeses— ah, the cheeses—all four aisles full of them. As the few remaining days in Savonnieres start to tick away, we're left to wish that the clock would stop, or at least that these friends will regroup to vacation again maybe next time in Italy or Spain or again in France."   —*The Union Leader*, Manchester, NH

"Haller's new book is a wonderful blend of the story of his trip, the lore of France, and the value of close friends and, of course, good food. . . . Ideal for armchair travelers, Francophiles, cooks, and any-one who has dreamed of a similar trip, *Vie de France* delights the senses. . . . James Haller inspires readers to invite friends over to share good times over a delectable meal—and that, Haller would insist, is what life is all about."   —*Dover Community News*

"James Haller makes the reader feel like a welcomed, coddled, and well-fed seventh guest during his dream-come-true stay at Savonnieres in the heart of the Loire Valley."   —Susan Simon, author of *The Nantucket Table*

"An elegant tribute to friendship and joie de vivre that France still offers. Refreshingly, Haller is as much intent on celebrating friendship as the good life abroad."   —*Kirkus Reviews*

"The key to this uplifting biographical month is how important friendship is to the human condition . . . an inspirational toast to the stimulation of camaraderie that is a human need in order to live precious life to the fullest."   —*BookBrowser*

Vie de France

SHARING FOOD, FRIENDSHIP,
AND A KITCHEN
IN THE LOIRE VALLEY

JAMES HALLER

Berkley Books, New York

A Berkley Book
Published by The Berkley Publishing Group
A division of Penguin Group (USA) Inc.
375 Hudson Street
New York, New York 10014

Copyright © 2002 by James Haller
Text design by Tiffany Kukec
Cover design by Brad Springer

PRINGING HISTORY
Berkley hardcover edition / June 2002
Berkley trade paperback edition / June 2003

Berkley trade paperback edition ISBN: 0-425-19011-0

The Library of Congress has catalogued the Berkley hardcover edition as follows:

Haller, James.
Vie de France : sharing food, friendship, and a kitchen in the Loire Valley / James Haller.
p. cm.
ISBN 0-425-18472-2
1. Cookery, French. I. Title.

TX719 .H2637 2002
641.5944—dc21
2001052927

Printed in the United States of America

10 9 8 7 6 5 4 3 2 1

Dedicated with grateful fondness to
J. and C.M. for their lovely house

≈

and the friendly people of Savonnieres

≈

and, of course, le Club Français

Acknowledgments

I would like to credit John Byrne, who collaborated with me on this effort and whose keen observations and editing acumen helped to bring this book to life.

I would like to thank Anne Sauve for her editing skills; Eve Corey for her supportive and sympathetic reading of an early draft; and Steve and Diane McHenry, Noella Tripetti, Norman Martinen, Reid McHenry, Bruce Teatreau and Lynn Pichette for their valued friendship. I would also like to mention Steve and Rene du Bois of Computer Concepts in Dover, New Hampshire, whose patient instruction kept me from smashing my laptop and printer against the wall on more than one occasion.

Table of Menus

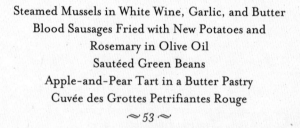

Steamed Mussels in White Wine, Garlic, and Butter
Blood Sausages Fried with New Potatoes and
Rosemary in Olive Oil
Sautéed Green Beans
Apple-and-Pear Tart in a Butter Pastry
Cuvée des Grottes Petrifiantes Rouge
~ 53 ~

Chowder Français with Croutons Provençal
Strawberries with Crème Fraîche
Chilled Vouvray
~ 62 ~

Peach Crepes with Homemade Strawberry Sauce
~ 64 ~

Moroccan Olive Salad
~ 68 ~

Cassoulet with Sausage and Soissons
Vanilla Apple Tart
~ 72 ~

TABLE OF MENUS

Pleurette Omelet
Toasted Baguette with Emmenthal
～ 74 ～

Roast Chicken Stuffed with Cassoulet
Apricot Lavender Tart
～ 82 ～

Tagliatelli with Roasted Peppers in a Red Wine Tomato Sauce
Stuffed Eggplant
Poire Williams Sorbet
Gold-Dipped Chocolate Almonds
1996 Chinon
～ 90 ～

Baguette French Toast with an Apricot Sauce
～ 94 ～

Tsatziki and Mixed Salad
1996 Vin d'Alsace Reisling
～ 96 ～

Chicken Vegetable Soup with Homemade Noodles
Strawberries with Sugar and Crème Fraîche
～ 99 ～

Sausage and Red Wine Ragout
Baguettes
Chocolate with Hazelnuts
～ 106 ～

———

TABLE OF MENUS

Mousse de Canard
Avocado, Ripe Tomatoes, and Onion Salad
Celeriac Rémoulade
Camembert and Chèvre
Baguettes
Petits Suisses with Ripe Peaches
Sparkling Vouvray
~ 109 ~

Turkey Cutlets Baked in a White Wine and
Emmenthal Cream Sauce
New Potatoes Fried with Cabbage
Green Beans Sautéed in Garlic and Olive Oil
Fresh Strawberries on Vanilla Ice Cream
Kir Royales
~ 114 ~

White Sausage Ragout with Red Wine, Basil, and Garlic
Chocolate
Espresso
1996 Vin de Pays de l'Agenais Cabernet Sauvignon
~ 122 ~

Roasted Herb Chicken
Pasta in a White Wine and Bell Pepper Sauce
Curried Peach-and-Pear Orange Custard Tart
~ 125 ~

Chicken Pasta Salad
Camembert with Baguettes
Chocolate Hazelnut Bars
~ 129 ~

TABLE OF MENUS

TABLE OF MENUS

Prologue

I NEVER THOUGHT I'D BE A COOK.

At age twenty-three I left Chicago for New York City with the dream of pursuing a career in writing and show business. Noël Coward and Cole Porter were my idols. Their sophisticated lyrics and soigné celebrity style set the standard of an ambition for which, I can see now, I—as a high school dropout and missing a couple of front teeth—was wholly unsuited.

Nevertheless, I managed to write the lyrics and book for a two-act musical, *The Ladies of Bank Street*, which actually had producers interested, and I sold a couple of skits for a review at a place called the Upstairs at the Downstairs. In one, Lily Tomlin played a girl who comes to New York to become a waitress and can only get a job as a star. One summer I played stock at a barn theater in Connecticut, where I wrote a musical parody of *Psycho* and played Norman Bates singing (as his mother) in a falsetto reminiscent of Ethel Merman.

All this was great fun, but of course didn't pay the rent. And so, unlike Lily Tomlin's would-be waitress, I had come to New York to be a star and could only find work as a waiter. I bounced in and out of several eateries, did a stint with the Arthur Treacher Butler Service, and by 1966, as I was turning thirty, I landed at Chumley's in the heart of the Village. There, working three nights a week, I could take home almost two hundred dollars. In those long-ago days, my rent on a five-room railroad apartment on the Upper East Side, Ninetieth Street, was only ninety dollars a month.

By the summer of 1968, *Hair* was setting the trend for musical theater and *The Ladies of Bank Street* seemed out of the times. I quietly put it aside, grew a mustache, stopped cutting my hair, and donned several strands of beads, which, on occasion, would hang in someone's dinner order and collect a little gravy.

"Oh, sorry, man . . ."

"Hey, I'm cool with it . . ."

It was the sixties.

I formed a rock group with four other people and began writing what I thought was sophisticated folk. We called our group the Flossie Hollihan and played the Village Gate . . . once.

I went back to Chumley's.

"Man, what's on your beads?"

"Gravy."

"I can dig it."

That was the sixties.

~ ~ ~

ONE DAY THE FENDER guitarist invited me to meet his guru, a charismatic and beautiful Dutch woman in her mid-sixties who held weekly theosophical discussions in her living room. She said that I was "afraid of success" and gave me a small piece of lapis lazuli on a chain, which she said had the power to "ward off the fear of good things happening to me." I immediately put the lapis around my neck.

At this time my old friend Gene, from my Chicago days, was living in New Hampshire directing children's theater with a Title III project called TRY—Theater Resources for

Youth—one of LBJ's "Great Society" programs. He was renting a wonderful house in Dover, with a huge fireplace, a loft bedroom, a small kitchen, and a tiny guest bedroom, where I stayed during my frequent visits. Frequent because in the sixties you could fly from La Guardia to Boston between eleven and two in the afternoon for eleven dollars.

I loved the nearby seaside town of Portsmouth, New Hampshire, from the moment I first saw it. I loved the dignity of its eighteenth- and nineteenth-century homes, the narrow streets, ancient trees, and its granite embankment along the Piscataqua, which divides New Hampshire from Maine.

I had wanted to live in Maine ever since I was a kid in the early forties and saw an ad on a Chicago bus advertising Alka-Seltzer. It read: "From Maine to California more people choose Alka-Seltzer" and had, on one side, a picture of a little boy in a stocking cap standing next to a pine tree on a snow-capped hill, and on the other, a lady at the beach in a bathing suit sitting under an umbrella wearing sunglasses. Maine definitely looked more attractive.

And so, in the spring of 1969, I quit my job, sublet my apartment, and moved into a little schoolhouse I rented about ten miles outside of Portsmouth, across the river in Maine. Built in 1820, the house was rustic but well appointed. It had a fireplace, a sink with hot water, blue wainscoting with white plaster walls in the sitting room, red and white in the kitchen. There was a cookstove and a woodstove, an outhouse, and I had to go skinny-dipping in the Great Works river down the hill when I wanted to take a bath. I slept in the attic on a mattress. Best of all, it was only twenty-five dollars a month, which, when subtracted from the sublet, left me enough to live on.

I spent that summer working on my first book (an autobiographical memoir: *Do You Need Me?*), swimming in the river, and spending an occasional afternoon at nearby Ogunquit Beach. It was there, one day in early August, that I met Mark, the young man who was to become my future business partner.

"Excuse me," he asked as I walked by, pointing to the piece of lapis, "why do you wear a blue strawberry around your neck?"

We instantly became good friends, and by October, the two of us returned to New York City, when, much to my amazement, I was signed to a name talent agency after some of my material had been well received on Johnny Carson's *Tonight Show* and *The Merv Griffin Show*. I sent them everything I thought was worthwhile, including *The Ladies of Bank Street* and my newly finished autobiography. Feeling myself on the eve of success but still needing to pay the rent, I took another job as a waiter while Mark kept books for an art-glass company. All through that fall and winter the agency responded to my inquiries with further reassurances. Things were about to happen.

In May, a new landlord, anxious to turn my five rooms

into three studio apartments, at six times the rent I had been paying, offered to buy out the lease at a price that seemed too good to refuse. The future felt secure. We sold the flat, quit our jobs, moved back to Maine and the schoolhouse, and waited for things to happen.

It was a beautiful summer. We planted an enormous garden and proudly raised broccoli, brussels sprouts, eggplant, corn, potatoes, tomatoes, and string beans in bucolic retreat while I awaited my first writing assignment.

One afternoon, the mail arrived and with it all the material I had turned into the agency with a terse little note: "We do not feel at this time that you are salable."

The entire dream crumbled. Writing for television, buying the lovely country house, driving the Porsche, flying off periodically to the West Coast to be met by limousines from the big networks all suddenly disappeared. With the rejected pages cradled in my arms, I sat down in the middle of the eggplant patch to consider my desperate situation. Looking toward heaven, I announced, "I'm at the end of my rope." And, as if in response to my declaration, there abruptly followed the best advice I have ever given myself: "Well then, dummy, let go!"

Through what proved to be a paradoxically fortuitous coincidence of misfortunes, my friend Gene also found himself suddenly without an income when the budget for the Title III programs was abruptly canceled at this time. Gene, Mark, and I were commiserating together at Gene's house not long afterward. I was thinking I could wait tables again, although, with fall approaching and the summer restaurants closing for the season, the timing was inauspicious. Gene might have gotten a job teaching, but it was already too late to land anything other than a substitute position. Neither of us was very enthused about these prospects.

"Why don't we open a restaurant?" Mark proposed jokingly. "At least that way we'd always eat."

"Can I be the cook?" I asked, not entirely certain if the proposal was a joke.

Cooking has always been something for which I felt an innate confidence. When I was ten months old, my mother brought me to work with her in the tearoom where she was a waitress. I would sit in my high chair in the kitchen, near the cook, and he'd give me food to play with all morning long—carrots and mashed potatoes, some peas, maybe a piece of celery. Food has been a toy in my life ever since.

Cooking is a sixth sense that has never failed to inform me what the next step is. When I was two and a half years old, I got up early one morning and, while my parents still slept, mixed together a dozen eggs (with their shells), a bag of flour, and a quart of milk with the intention of making pancakes. What I made was a mess! But the thing to look at here is that I got all the ingredients right.

For years, I had enjoyed throwing impromptu dinner parties for my friends, instinctively putting together dishes like Cornish hens in a sour-cream-and-sherry sauce with carroway; or ham baked in fresh raspberries with Grand Marnier; or a dish called Noodles High, improvised one night from what I had left in the cupboards: noodles, sour cream, buttermilk, half a jar of grated Parmesan, a hit of cognac, a lot of garlic, and some dried basil. But this was the first time I had ever thought about cooking for a living.

Throughout the afternoon we continued discussing the restaurant with growing excitement. What had begun as an offhand proposal was contemplated as a real possibility, and before we had left Gene's house that evening, had emerged as the solution to all our problems.

I had eaten at a restaurant in New York called Casa Brazil, where dinner was served in two seatings, one at seven P.M., the other at nine, and I was so impressed with their system that I advocated our own restaurant be run on the same premise. This was an undertaking I felt I could handle. I would simply be cooking a wonderful dinner twice a night.

Undaunted by our lack of funds, we began evolving a plan of action. First we drew up a list of everything we thought we would need and assessed a start-up cost of about forty-five hundred dollars. Gene's brother-in-law lent him fifteen hundred dollars and Mark and I borrowed our share from two friends. Even before finding a location, we began perusing the numerous secondhand shops in and around Portsmouth. I found two archaic apartment-size stoves for fifteen dollars apiece, two twenty-year-old refrigerators for another thirty dollars, and pots and pans and kettles for under ten dollars for the lot. We bought forty unmatched pressed wood dining-room chairs for two and a half dollars apiece. Dinner plates, cake plates, and dessert plates were had for a quarter each, bread-and-butter-size dishes for a dime. We bought white dimestore mugs for soups and coffee, and new tables so that they would all be the same size. A friend who worked for Wedgwood gave us forty sample plates, which we used as underliners. Beautiful old platters could be had for two and three dollars. Gene's house had become a mini storage center.

One morning, driving along Ceres Street, a block-long alley squeezed between eighteenth-century warehouses and tugboats, we noticed a crew replacing a floor in the basement of an old granary. Looking in through the window, we found bare brick walls, a beamed ceiling, and a fireplace with an impressive rough-hewn mantel. It seemed to be everything we could hope for as a location for the resturaunt and we went inside to inquire about renting it. The foreman turned out to be the owner of the building. He was interested to hear our plan, and the next day, November 2, 1970, offered us a lease.

The landlord installed spiderweb sconces, all the electrical fixtures, the bathrooms, dark red carpeting, and built walls to separate the kitchen area from the dining room. What wasn't brick we painted a flat white, with all the woodwork in Wedg-wood blue. A friend who owned an antique store lent us several beautiful paintings, filling the spaces between the sconces with gilt-framed American landscapes and portraits.

In the deep recess of the front window, looking across the alley to a view of the tugs and the river, we placed two hand-carved wooden figures—a drummer and a cymbal player—that had once fit on the side of a calliope. For the fireplace we had found sand-cast andirons in the shape of maidens.

Everything fell into place so easily! The town and state officials with whom we dealt couldn't have been more helpful. Even the liquor commission bent over backward accommodating the liquor laws to the (then) novel concept of two nightly seatings. Previously, in order to get a liquor license you had to serve both lunch and dinner with eight choices of entrées at each meal.

Gene sent announcements I had composed to all the businesses in a thirty-mile radius culled from several phone books, and we were sold out three days before opening night.

On November 18, at the remarkable cost of only twenty-seven hundred dollars in total, we opened to a full house. We called it Blue Strawbery with only one *r* in the *berry* in deference to the old way of spelling Strawbery Banke, the original name for Portsmouth.

The fact that before this evening I had never cooked for more than eight people never fazed me. I made a list of all the dishes I knew how to cook and created the opening-night menu from it: a hot vichyssoise; artichoke hearts in a white wine cream sauce; crab-stuffed mushrooms; salad with a frozen cranberry dressing; tenderloin of beef in red wine and mushrooms; carrots in curry and honey; potatoes roasted in garlic; zucchini in dill and butter; and string beans fried in bacon. Unskilled in desserts, I heaped fresh strawberries on a platter with a mound of brown sugar and a pile of sour cream—the routine being to dip the strawberry into the sour cream, then into the brown sugar, and eat. It became our hallmark dessert.

Dinner began promptly at eight and ended at one-fifteen in the morning, to a round of applause. We were an immediate sensation. The local newspapers raved about the new restaurant in Portsmouth and "Chef" Haller's amazing cuisine.

It all seemed so unreal to me. Since I had never formally studied cooking or even followed recipes, the title *chef* seemed almost illegitimate. I felt that I had never worked hard enough to acquire this knowledge, which, to me, appeared to be just a talent for making food taste good. More importantly, I was having a terrific time. How could anything that was this much fun be work?

Having never formally studied cooking, I was unbound by any of the preconceived rules about what you should or should not do, and so, as long as the food tasted great, I never felt as though I was doing anything wrong. No one ever said no to me. No one ever told me I was doing something incorrectly or that I *shouldn't* do something. Gene and Mark were perfect business partners, never questioning anything I wanted to do in the kitchen. This gave me complete freedom to be creative. Like doors flying open, wild ideas of concoctions and mixes of tastes flooded my imagination and every day I cooked something new, never repeating a menu, trying never to repeat a dish. It was art, like painting, like composing. Creating a fine meal was an instant artistic achievment, eliciting an instant reaction that continued to motivate me to rampant innovation. Cooking was, and still is, a kind of magic to me. The fusion of herbs and wines that turns duck or veal, fish or pheasant, into a taste that thrills the palate is an amazing feat of alchemy.

One evening in January, just a month and a half after we had opened, a blizzard had canceled out all our reservations. The candles were still lit in the window and the three of us were about to put everything away for the night when there was a knock on the door. I opened to a party of six people who asked, "Are you a restaurant?" We assured them that we were, invited them in, and fed them. At the end of the meal they explained they were from *Boston* magazine and had been up to Kennebunkport, Maine, earlier in the day to do a story on a restaurant that had turned out so disappointing they hadn't even finished the meal. Excited by my cooking, they asked permission to do a story on us, and of course we agreed. A few weeks later the cover of the magazine featured the headline FOR A GREAT DINNER IN BOSTON DRIVE TO PORTSMOUTH, NEW HAMPSHIRE, AND BLUE STRAWBERY.

With that boost, and the brilliant press kits that Gene continued mailing out in that first year, we were soon receiving dinner reservations months in advance from all over the country. People would call from California or Utah or Ohio and say, "We're going to be in New England this summer, can we make reservations for August?" New Year's Eve, Thanksgiving, and Easter would fill up a year in advance. It was truly the beginning of a career I had never even considered.

All through the seventies and into the eighties, our reputation continued to grow. I was still loving the kitchen, still passionate about the creation of new dishes. The restaurant had become my whole world, the people who worked there my family. However, at the same time, relations between the three of us partners had begun to deteriorate. Mark and I had long since severed our domestic relationship, but had never resolved the antagonizing conflicts that had led to the break, and they continued poisoning the partnership for us both.

By 1986, our estrangement finally reached a crisis, dissolving the partnership just before my fiftieth birthday. I simultaneously suffered the end of a long relationship and the death of my dog. My life was sounding like a country-and-western song. The legal proceedings to sell out my share of the corporation became protracted and ugly. It took over a year and a half to be definitively settled, and during this time Mark died of cancer.

Meanwhile, I had opened a little charcuterie that failed miserably but, from it, had evolved a business preparing "entrées to go" out of my home three days a week for a local produce market and specialty deli that carried imported cheeses and wines. At the same time, I was invited to be guest chef at the Shaker Village in Canterbury, New Hampshire. I worked at the Village for a year and a half and left to concentrate on my third cookbook, an improvisation on traditional Shaker recipes.

I continued doing the food for "takeout" for the next several years, during which time I published my fourth and fifth books. My cooking had changed once again. Now it was more simple, more recognizable. I was making platters of stuffed cabbage like my grandmother used to make, casseroles with sausage and potatoes and sauerkraut, macaroni with three cheeses, and old-fashioned potato pancakes. People loved it, but I felt unfulfilled in the preparation; it all had become lackluster, simply a job in which I no longer felt inspired. A cold case in the deli section was not as grand a stage as the beautiful dining room of my restaurant.

I had been cooking for almost thirty years professionally and it is a profession I truly love. But in the past few years the tedium of the kitchen, the sameness of the venue, had made the work seem mundane. Food, and the process of cooking, had never for an instant lost its appeal, yet of late, in the storehouse of my imagination, there didn't seem to be anything left.

It was 1996 and I was about to turn sixty years old—a sobering age. I wanted the security of old friends to reassure me that I hadn't changed (too much) from that bearded, long-haired guy who lit the fire in his kitchen almost thirty years before. I wanted to cook a wonderful dinner to celebrate. I wanted a birthday party.

Little did I know it would launch the next great adventure of my life.

The Birthday Party

THE CAKE WAS A SENSATION. A CHOCOLATE, FOUR-layered génoise filled with raspberries and chocolate ganache, covered with a hazelnut cream and decorated with hand-painted buttercream grapes and leaves. Jack had purchased it from one of the most reknowned French pastry chefs in New

Hampshire. Mona, Helmut, Madeline, and Mackie lit the candles. While everyone sang "Happy Birthday," I closed my eyes and made the same silent wish I had always made: that this would be a year of fulfillment, the beginning of the most wonderful time of my life. To everyone's amazement, including mine, I blew out all sixty candles in a single breath.

Over coffee, the topic of conversation turned to a mutual acquaintance who was spending a year in the south of France.

"I would love to rent a house someplace," I said. "Maybe France or Italy, and stay for an extended length of time . . . you know, a month in one place, instead of running from city to city every couple of days." People agreed it was the way to see Europe.

"It would be wonderful." Madeline sighed, as if it were a distant and impossible dream. "Imagine, finding a beautiful house in some wonderful place and just living there for a whole month."

"Well, why *can't* we do that?" Mona demanded as the last bottle of wine was emptied into a round of glasses. "We *could* do that." There was a certain bravado in her insistence, brought on by the wine and the festivities, which gave her statement the aura of a dare.

"Okay," I said, accepting the challenge. "You put it together and we'll do it."

Everyone thought it was a great idea. Jokingly we discussed the question of places to go. "How about Tuscany?"

"Oh, everyone is going to Italy," I said in mock snobbery. "We'd run into nothing but Americans."

"Spain?"

"Spain is beautiful, but you never know when to eat!" I pleaded. "I was always too late for breakfast, too late for lunch, and too early for dinner."

"That's true," Madeline chimed in. "They eat very late."

"They don't eat dinner until ten o'clock at night!" I continued. "The only thing I want at that hour is two rolls and a turnover."

People groaned.

Mackie suggested Portugal, which was inexpensive, but no one seemed to know much about the place. Jack thought England might be nice. "But it's expensive," somebody said.

"How about Nome?" Helmut offered. "I'll bet that's cheap."

"That's just what I want after a long New England winter," Madeline replied, feigning enthusiasm, "a whole month in Alaska. Why not Ghana?"

The suggestions continued like a silly game until the humor, like the wine, began to run out.

"You know, I'm really serious," Mona again insisted. "We could do this. Let's all find a house someplace in Europe and go for a month."

There was a short silence. The six of us looked around the table at one another and nodded okay in conditional agreement. The "conditions," of course, being *if* we could get away from work, *if* we could take the time, and *if* we had the money. Mostly it was if we had the money, since at this point we had no idea what this venture might cost. While none of us was living on the edge, we were not people with stock portfolios that had already ensured us a comfortable retirement. We needed to find someplace affordable.

But as much as I loved the idea of spending time in Europe, I had my doubts it would ever happen. It was the sort of spur-of-the-moment enthusiasm that, in my life, frequently collapsed before the reality could take hold. But our game was slowly evolving from fantasy to reality. We continued to discuss the questions of time, place, and money without resolution, finally agreeing to meet again to elaborate on our plan.

Before we said good night, we lifted what remained in our glasses in a final toast. "Here's to Europe. May it be everything we want it to be!"

"I'm not cooking," I said sternly. "I'm not lifting a pot for the entire month."

I can't speak for the others, but what I wanted Europe to be was beautiful scenery, peace and quiet, my own bathroom, and definitely no cooking.

≈ ≈ ≈

WITH THE EXCEPTION OF Jack, with whom I have lived for fourteen years, and Helmut, who had more recently come into our lives after he and Madeline bought a house together, I had known the others for almost a quarter of a century. In the years that we were establishing Blue Strawbery, Mona and Madeline, childhood friends, were attending the state university at nearby Durham, New Hampshire. After graduating, they moved to Maine to a somewhat derelict but beautifully situated old Cape Cod on a high bank of the Piscataqua just up and across the river from Portsmouth. Mona eventually purchased the house. In those days, Portsmouth and its surrounding area was a remarkably inexpensive place to buy or rent, and this contributed to a vibrant local arts scene.

I first knew Madeline as a talented performer in a dance company to which my partners and I had contributed efforts at fund-raising. Through her I was introduced to Mona. On occasion they would wait tables in my restaurant. I was very fond of them both. Unfortunately, as time went on, I saw less of them than I would have liked. When Mona and Mackie, whom I knew less well, were married, they moved to Boston, where he worked for an architectural firm, while Mona was employed in the art department of a publishing house. Already in their late thirties when their son, Rory, was conceived, and not wishing to raise a child in the city, Mona and Mackie returned to the little house in Maine. From the mid-eighties on, I began running into them around town again, often accompanied by Rory, whom I remember as a blond-headed baby in OshKosh B'Gosh overalls. Mackie had taken a less glamorous job with an engineering firm, and he and

Mona began a collaboration that transformed the little house into one of the most appealing and comfortable homes I know.

It was at their home that we met for dinner again sometime in early February to continue discussing the proposed trip. This time we succeeded in outlining the dimensions a little more concretely. We agreed that the coming summer didn't give us enough time to plan and settled for a year from that summer. I had convinced Jack to commit to a full month's stay. Mona also wished to stay the entire month. Helmut and Madeline would only be staying for the first two weeks, since the summer is the busiest time for the airport shuttle service they own and manage together, and they felt unable to be away for any longer. Mackie and Rory would be arriving for the final two.

Even as we discussed these arrangements, the trip remained a far-off dream of adventure we animatedly discussed, but that I never thought would actually happen.

～ ～ ～

THROUGHOUT THAT WINTER AND into the following spring and summer, we continued meeting periodically for dinner. If nothing else ever came from it, it was a perfect excuse to get together with a party of amiable people.

Sometime later that spring, Mona, who was now teaching junior-high-school art classes, invited Eve, a colleague, to one of our dinners. A sociology and history teacher, Eve is a gifted painter and proved an enlivening addition to the group, which she began referring to as le Club Français. Later that winter she asked to join our expedition, but felt unable to commit to longer than a week's stay. Her longtime companion, Molly, a basset hound, was old and not in the best of health, and Eve feared leaving her alone any longer than a week might prove disastrous.

I don't recall exactly when it was that Lettie, Mona's sister, joined the plans, but I think it must have been sometime that summer. It was through her that we found the house that would so beautifully accommodate us. A coworker told her of a house she had rented somewhere in the French countryside in a little town called Savonnieres.

Surfing on the Web, Rory discovered that Savonnieres was about a hundred and thirty miles south of Paris. Consulting an atlas, we found the town just below the city of Tours in the region of Touraine, the heart of the Loire Valley, where royalty had, most famously, built their châteaux—a region known as "the Garden of France."

After a phone call to the company that managed the property, we received a package of information.

The black-and-white Xeroxed photos were less than impressive and even a little disappointing, but the description of the house, which boasted three bedrooms with three baths and a study with its own bathroom and sofabed, met the most important requirements. As close as we had all become in these months of planning, no one wanted to think of nine people sharing one bathroom, doubling up in bedrooms, or sleeping on sofas. Best of all, at five thousand dollars for the month, the weekly rental cost came to twelve hundred and fifty dollars. Since there would never be less than six people living in the house, the cost split six ways came to two hundred and eight dollars apiece. This fell well within our price range.

It was evident we could not afford to rent a chateau, but as long as the place was clean, comfortable, and (fairly) respectable, we would be happy. It seemed a simple decision for us to make. Mona contacted the people who managed the property. The month that we requested, July 15 to August 15, was available, and the next time we gathered we collected the down payment. With a surge of elation I wrote out a check for my share. It was the first piece of documentation attesting to our tenancy of a house in another country.

It was Mona who assumed the management of everything having to do with the particulars of the house: collecting our checks, mailing them off to the right place, even the arrangements for a rental car.

That fall, Manuel, a friend of Mackie's, came to one of our dinners to show us his slides of France. An artist and painter in his late forties, Manuel is also a carpenter, a skill he was exchanging for the use of an apartment in Paris at the same time that we were planning our own trip, and we looked forward to seeing him in France.

By January, the final payments were made and we were

sent another packet of information with instructions telling us where to get the train in Paris, at what station to get off, how to get to Savonnieres, where the keys to the house would be, and whom to call when we finally arrived.

Even as the plan began to finalize, I still questioned the actuality of this happening. I could hardly believe it wasn't going to fall apart at any moment. Jokingly we suggested different scenarios. "Maybe this is all a French scam and somebody had all this stuff printed up and photographs made, and now that they've taken our money, the house won't exist."

"Suppose when we get there the place turns out to be a shambles and there's only one bedroom and the toilet is outside!" Helmut speculated. It was my ultimate nightmare.

By the end of June, Eve sadly and suddenly had to back out of the plan. Molly was not doing well. It was a concern and a disappointment to all. As for the rest of us, Mona, Lettie, Jack, and I would be arriving on the sixteenth of July and staying until the fifteenth of August. Having found a charter flight on the Internet that would save a couple hundred dollars, Helmut and Madeline were arriving for their two-week stay a few days after us. Rory and his father, Mackie, after a short stop in London, where they would visit Lettie's daughter, Agnes, would be arriving for the final two weeks. Excepting a two-day overlap between their arrival and Madeline and Helmut's departure, the sleeping arrangements worked out perfectly.

By the first of July, my lingering sense of doubt exploded into panic. We were actually going.

Arriving in France

I HAVE A LITTLE PROBLEM WITH FLYING. NOTHING serious. It's just that I burst into tears the minute the plane leaves the ground and I weep for the entire flight. It's somewhat embarrassing. Usually the flight attendants quickly form one of those bereavement support groups that have become so

popular and try to console me, assuming there's been a loss in the family. When I tell them I'm simply terrified, they shun me for the rest of the trip and I become too embarrassed even to ask for extra peanuts. As a result of this phobia, I had for years been enduring the nightmares of driving or taking a train on long trips, two forms of traveling in the United States that in terms of comfort, convenience, and safety are rivaled only by their equivalents in third-world countries. Neither of these forms of transportation was an option for passing over the Atlantic. I had to fly.

I spoke to my doctor and asked (read *begged*) if he might prescribe enough tranquilizers to get me there and back. I simply could not endure a vacation that began and ended with seven hours of nonstop weeping.

At last the day arrived. Half dazed from the excitement (and a little Valium, I admit) I arrived with my friends at Logan Airport two hours in advance, as instructed, to begin the check-in process. As a consequence of its perpetual renovations, the airport was in chaos—streets blocked, concrete dividers everywhere, no place to park for even a moment, and the ubiquitous police ordering everyone to "move on!" Mackie pulled the car over to the curb, quickly hugged Mona good-bye, and we hastily yanked our suitcases from the trunk before the scowling policeman heading our way could give him a ticket. Like refugees from a repressive dictatorship rushing for the last opportunity to freedom, we sped into the relative quiet of the terminal.

We had already checked our luggage in when I realized I had left my Valium in my suitcase and, panic-stricken, on the verge of tears, went frantically running after the baggage man, whom I tipped generously to pull my bag. At last Jack, Mona, and I boarded the plane, fastened our seat belts, and at 6:10 on the evening of July 15, just as we had planned, lifted into the sky and headed for France.

We left Boston while it was still light, flew into the evening, then through the darkness of night and into the European dawn, landing at Orly at 7:00 A.M., French time. Conveniently, Lettie was scheduled to arrive from Ohio within the hour.

Up until this time I had been thinking, Suppose we don't like Lettie . . . After all, she had never been a part of our dinners together, and even though she had been instrumental in realizing our plan, we really knew her only through Mona. Maybe she was one of those people who was a know-it-all and spoke French all the time and would ridicule us when we faltered through it. But when she appeared dragging a suitcase, waving and laughing as she headed toward us, I felt instantly that we would like each other.

Outside the airport, we hailed a cab large enough for the four of us and our suitcases. Imagine my shock when the driver actually got out, took our bags, and put them into the trunk. I marveled at this strange custom of helpful cabdrivers, as we drove through Paris, gray and overcast with a slight drizzle. The radio was playing Andrea Bocelli singing "Time to Say

Goodbye." It was so romantic that we were hushed for practically the entire ride.

At the Gare d' Austerlitz, the driver once again helped Jack and me with the luggage while Lettie and Mona, following the directions that had been sent, procured second-class tickets for us to a place called St.-Pierre-des-Corps. A short time later we boarded and the train pulled away from the Parisian mist and headed south. The farther we traveled from the city, the sunnier it became. Within an hour, we were passing through fields of the most golden grain and hay I had ever seen, and past endless stretches of sunflowers all in bloom—thousands upon thousands of intense yellow faces looking up at the sun. On the back roads and in small villages, we could see stone houses, dusty gray in color, with brick-tiled or slate roofs that swooped from the top right down to the foundations.

The gentle rocking of the train could easily have induced us to close our eyes but then, across the aisle, a child began talking excitedly and pointing to the fields. Craning our necks, we saw our first château in the distance. A vision of beauty and grace, sitting on a far hillside, like a palace in a fairy tale, it nudged a pleasure from my childhood that had long since slipped from memory.

I suddenly had this strange feeling that I was about to fall in love.

≈ ≈ ≈

TWO AND A HALF hours later, the train slowed and somewhere in the mystery of the conductor's language we deciphered "St.-Pierre-des-Corps!"

There we were, a little punchy from no sleep but still enthusiastic, dragging our baggage out of a train station somewhere in France, with no real grasp of the language, not exactly certain where we were, and only the vaguest idea of where we were heading, how we were going to get there, or how long it would take.

It was exhilarating.

We headed toward the car-rental agency just outside the station, and to our great disappointment, they were locked up tight. The exhilaration began to wane slightly.

Over the previous months, Mona and Lettie had made dozens of phone calls to St.-Pierre-des-Corps, haggling in English and French about the cost and size of a car—which changed each time they talked with someone new. Phoning back and forth to each other between calls to France, often on the verge of tears while relating each new price quotation, they had come precariously close to nervous breakdowns, but at long last, they were promised a "big" car for a reasonable price. To arrive and find the rental agency closed after all of that seemed a tremendous setback. The four of us stood there in front of the closed office, stymied.

Noticing our dilemma, a passerby informed us that with the exception of restaurants, everyone closed for lunch from noon to two.

A two-hour lunch? How civilized is that? I thought.

"You know," Mona said, her disappointment transforming into need for food, "I'm hungry. Can we eat?"

A few doors down from the rental agency was a small restaurant. Inside, the hostess gestured to a convenient luggage rack and, after we had stored our suitcases, showed us to our table. Unaffected and gracious, her manner allayed our apprehensions about the car. Here we were, having a little glitch in the travel plans and a charming stranger was being perfectly lovely to us.

I had the distinct feeling France was flirting with me.

I ordered a salade niçoise and a glass of white wine of the region. We relaxed into our first meal in France together. Oddly enough, after no sleep for several hours and all of the traveling from Maine to Boston to Orly to Paris to at last this place, the four of us seemed simply and genuinely happy. Sitting and grinning at one another, eating great food, sipping white wine in the afternoon, devouring a baguette, and drinking very black coffee, we congratulated ourselves for having actually pulled it off. Completely unaware of what this next month would bring, we grinned some more and just eased back. A couple smiled and nodded a *bonjour* as they passed our table. Across the street we could see boxes of flowers, dripping with color, beneath windows and on small balconies. Even the train station had been adorned with great cement planters filled with flowers like explosions of brilliance beneath the blue and cloudless sky.

For dessert, I had a slice of freshly baked tarte aux pommes.

France was definitely flirting.

~ ~ ~

BY THREE O'CLOCK, THE folks at the car rental were open. The manager, Bruno, began searching the computer for the agreement that had finally been settled on with Lettie, and after much conversation back and forth, uttered a *voilà* and printed out two copies of the contract. I handed him my credit card and began signing the papers. Smiling, he presented me with the keys. "*La grande Fiat blanche*," he declared.

Outside on the street, as we were attempting to figure out which *blanche* and *grande* Fiat he was talking about (it seemed as if half the cars in France were white and the other half Fiats), Bruno knocked on the window, pointing to a diminutive "square-back" parked nearest to the agency. The *grande* car turned out to be this very *petite* four-seater. We waved our thanks, piled our luggage into the trunk, and took our places. Both Lettie and Mona had neglected to bring their driver's licenses, and Jack feels about driving the same way I feel about flying.

Oh God, I thought, panicking. I'm actually going to have to drive a car in France!

In planning for this vacation, I had made two resolutions. The first was that I wasn't going to cook, and the second (given the reputation of French drivers) that I *definitely* was not driving anywhere for an entire month. I recalled this latter vow as I turned the key and pulled away from the curb. Noses buried deep in the directions that had been sent to us, Lettie and Mona began vociferating instructions from the backseat.

"As soon as you get over the bridge, look for Winston Churchill Boulevard, and make a right onto it."

"Turn here! Go straight! That's a red light . . . slow down . . . look out! . . . don't go over that bridge! You're driving too fast!" Dealing with French drivers, I quickly realized, was definitely not going to be the problem.

But I loved the little car. I enjoyed driving it from the moment I got behind the wheel. After I followed all of the street signs (and the directives from the backseat), within a half hour we saw the sign for Savonnieres and excitedly pulled into town.

We were immediately stopped by two policemen, who stood there, as if waiting for us, in the middle of the road. Visions of the Bastille danced through my head as I thought, This is the payoff. We're not here ten minutes and we've already broken the law.

"*Bonjour, monsieur,*" one of the officers said. Then he said something else I could not understand. There is, however, a sort of universal awareness at times like these. When someone in uniform is talking to you in a language you don't understand and carrying a gun, it's probably a pretty good idea to pull out any identification you have and present it. I opened the glove compartment, gave him the contract on the car, my driver's license, and my passport. He perused it all, bowed graciously, and said, *"Merci, monsieur, bon voyage."*

Confused but relieved, we began driving through town searching for the address where the instructions told us we would find the keys to our house.

"What do you think that was all about?" I asked, still a trifle uneasy about the encounter.

"Maybe we look like criminals." Mona thought it was funny.

"No, but we probably look like Americans," Jack offered.

"Well, we *have* been up all night," Lettie suggested as an excuse.

"Is this what the month is going to be like?" My question was glibly apprehensive.

As our directions promised, we soon arrived in front of a stone house that sat one step up from the edge of the street. Mona jumped out of the car, stood on the step, and knocked. We saw the door open but couldn't see the woman, only her outstretched hand as, a minute later, she handed Mona a bunch of keys.

"That was Madame Chinot," Mona informed us. "She said to turn around and go back to the main road, make a right, go another block and make a left, then follow it 'til you see the house."

I drove slowly (a dangerous move in France), searching the blue street signs for Rue de la Liberté.

The town of Savonnieres is small. One long street runs through the center along the Cher River, and from that street two or three narrow ones lead up the hill to stone houses built centuries ago. We gawked at everything—the houses, the streets, the river, the people, and the incredible abundance of flowers.

At long last we arrived at the gate of number 26 Rue de la Liberté.

≈ ≈ ≈

A HIGH ARCH CAPPED with terra-cotta tiles roofed the tall wooden gates to the drive. There was a smaller pedestrian entrance to their right. Mona got out, found the right keys, unlocked the gates, and swung them open. Across the street and a few houses down, a small brown, white, and black dog stood on a windowsill and yelled annoyingly at us.

Cautiously, I drove through and up the narrow drive as she closed the gates behind us. Lettie, Jack, and I climbed out of the little car and stood in silence surveying the destination of our year-and-a-half-long efforts. "Oh my." Smiles swiping across our faces, we sighed. "Look at this!"

The black-and-white Xeroxes hadn't even come close to doing it justice. A flowering wisteria covered the facing wall. Dahlias bloomed with a feathery pentstemon on the edge of a terrace tucked into a right angle formed by the ell that rambled from the front portion of the house right into the cliff face at the back of the garden. There were a number of caves in the cliffs; the first opening near the house served as a tool-shed, with a second for storing wine beside it, its smaller opening covered with a planked door painted bright red. A baking oven had also been carved into the cliffs (which were quite high, perhaps eighteen to twenty feet), and from the blackened stone above it I could surmise people had been cooking in it for hundreds of years.

In the back corner of the garden was the wall of the neigh-boring house, from which, intriguingly enough, several shin-like bones protruded out of the mortar. An eerie enigma to which we never found the explanation.

The garden was planted around the central axis of a rose *allée* underplanted with impatiens. In a vegetable plot, accented with topiaried boxwood, an abundance of dahlias were in flower. The retaining wall, which held the garden back from the street, rose up a few feet to a level with the eaves of the houses of our downhill neighbors, creating an enclosure of perfect privacy but open to a lovely view of the rooftops of Savonnieres.

Excitedly, we ascended the four steps up from the drive to the cobbled terrace. Built in 1680, the house is of gray lime-stone with deep-set casement windows that swing, doorlike, on hinges back into the rooms. Being from New England, we immediately noticed the absence of any screens. A large rose-bush, with medium-sized pink blossoms with just a tinge of apricot yellow, had been trained on the wall to frame one of the windows. On the other side of the terrace was the most remarkable boxwood tree I had ever seen. The trunk was a foot thick and the foliage, clipped in the shape of a giant gum-drop, formed an umbrella that captured shade and held it through the heat of the afternoon.

Unlocking the door, we entered the kitchen. A four-foot-high fireplace greeted us to the left, in front of which was a wood-plank dining table. To my surprise the kitchen boasted an electric convection oven with a gas-burner top, a food processor, a blender, good knives, good pots, pans, baking dishes, and a dishwasher. As I appreciatively assessed the kitchen, Mona and Lettie disappeared into the front of the house.

"Look at the size of the closets in this room!" I heard Lettie exclaiming as I followed Jack up the stone stairway that twisted out of the kitchen from the other side of the fireplace onto the second floor, where a steep-pitched hall led to the bedroom we were to occupy for the coming month. There was a large, comfortable bed, two chairs—one of them uphol-stered, a square bureau with four large drawers, and a mir-rored armoire occupying an entire wall. On one side of the room, the windows looked out over the terrace and into the garden. On the opposite wall, they opened over the rooftops of the neighbors across the street, to the river valley of fields and farms embraced by acres and acres of bright yellow sun-flowers.

Out in the hall a second door opened into a sunny, beauti-fully tiled bathroom. Viewing it, with its long, deep porcelain tub and hand shower, toilet, sink, and closet full of towels, I felt a great sense of relief wash over me.

≈ ≈ ≈

DOWNSTAIRS, WE FOLLOWED THE sound of Mona and Lettie's excited conversation toward the front of the house into a little hall just outside the kitchen. From there, a door opened out onto the terrace, with another bathroom beside it.

We found Lettie and Mona had already carried their baggage into the room they had selected. They were going to share the twin beds in one of the first-floor bedrooms, reserving the second downstairs bedroom for Madeline and Helmut, who were due to arrive in a couple of days. There were plush, thick draperies and a marble bust of a woman on the mantel. The beds were covered in a shimmering fabric, the floor entirely covered by carpet. In comparison to this luxury, our second-floor garret seemed almost austere.

Making our way back through the kitchen, together we entered an elegant, white-washed drawing room with a carved, bleached, stone fireplace. There was a wine-colored sofa and two Victorian "Venus de Milo" chairs (an upholstered back and seat but no arms), a thick carpet with a dark print over the stone floor, and on the walls, watercolors and an oil painting of a lush green landscape. In its entirety, the room was comfortably spectacular.

Behind the drawing room was the study, a little simpler in its furnishing, with two chairs, the pullout sofa, a writing desk, and a tiny black-and-white TV. The room also had its own bathroom and a door that opened onto the driveway near the first cave.

We worked our way back through the house a second time, opening and closing doors and cupboards, delighted at each turn of every corner. Everything—the beds, the chairs and tables, the entire house—was beautiful.

After we had unpacked, we called and introduced ourselves to Marie-Claire, (daughter-in-law to Madame Chinot), who the directions told us was the housekeeper, and then called the handyman, Monsieur Dumont, a retired railroad man who now managed his own vineyard. Both of them welcomed us and promised to come by the next day.

It was by now about five in the afternoon. We had all been up since six the previous morning and were becoming slightly numb, but we couldn't resist a quick walk just to see where we were. Following the narrow sidewalk down the short hill, we found ourselves in the center of town. We discovered a church, which was built in the twelfth century; two groceries; two patisseries—one at either end of the long street, both exhibiting beautiful pastries and breads; one charcuterie; a bureau de *poste*: a tabac; a boucherie; a pharmacie; and three cafés. Settling into one of the outside tables of the café across from the church, we ordered coffee and relaxed.

The road through town separated the café from a line of clipped linden trees running along the embankment where the tables were located, and the waitress had to dodge traffic to bring us the coffee. At our backs, the River Cher ran parallel to the main street. There was a small beach on the other side where people were swimming, some just lying on a dam sunning themselves in the shallow water that spilled over. Lettie commented that she was sorry she hadn't brought a bathing suit.

An older woman with a wonderful smile (brought on by one glass of wine too many) paused at our table and, in her native tongue, recommended another café just up the road—le Cheval Rouge, where, she assured us, the food was *très bien*. There was apparently some dispute between herself and the café owner, who appeared at the door and shouted at her to move on. Unfazed, she again welcomed us into town and continued weaving her way in and out of the shade trees.

We had lingered there for almost an hour when Jack suggested it was time we find something to eat for supper. No one wanted to even think about cooking that first night, so we stopped at the charcuterie. The aromas that greeted us as we stepped through the door brought smiles of delighted expectation to our faces. Among other delicious edible gifts and treats was a deli case of take-out food. Everything was so tempting it was difficult to make a choice. Our appetites building, we peered into the case, at last choosing the rillettes, a sort of shredded pork made from the head of a pig; salami; ratatouille, a baked mix of zucchini, summer squash, tomatoes, and onions; and celeriac rémoulade, shredded celery root in a creamy sauce of mayonnaise and Dijon mustard.

We also bought a baguette, two éclairs (one coffee and one chocolate), a small fruit tart, and a sort of chocolate box, the four corners pulled up like a handkerchief to the center at the top, filled with chocolate mousse and dusted with cocoa powder.

I could eat out of this store for the entire month, I thought, and not ever have to cook.

Back at the house we divided everything into fours and began gorging ourselves. The food was simply delicious. Between bites, our heads nodding, we giggled and drifted into short naps. We had all been up for over thirty-six hours. Mona put "Time to Say Goodbye" on the tape player. For me, it was time to say good night.

The bells from the church struck nine and it was still very light out. As exhausted as I was, I couldn't quite bring myself to the idea that we should retire for the night—it wasn't night yet. But we kept falling asleep at the table and finally had to drag ourselves off. The bed was large and so comfortable that the moment I put my head on the pillow, I was out, pleased that everyone had their own bedroom and bathroom.

"Fait accompli," I whispered, drifting off.

Friday, July 17

IT WAS AFTER TEN when we finally woke that first morning. I found half a bag of coffee in the refrigerator and plugged in the pot. My first taste of home-brewed French coffee. The strength was startling, like espresso. I loved it.

At the nearest boulangerie I got four croissants and a baguette, then stopped at the grocery and bought an eighth of a kilo of butter. When I returned, the others were up. I unwrapped the breakfast and we sat together at the kitchen table enjoying our first taste of French butter slathered over a crusty and still-warm baguette. It was as though I was eating butter for the first time.

Jack confessed he had slept fitfully, but Mona, Lettie, and I had rested soundly through to morning. Seated around the table, we savored our beautiful surroundings with a luxurious sense of the full month lying before us.

≈ ≈ ≈

AFTER BREAKFAST WE DECIDED we needed to buy a few groceries.

The owner of the house had thoughtfully put together a green-colored binder filled with information concerning the house and region, and for the first week we carried this valuable reference with us everywhere, citing "the green book" as the final arbiter of any question that arose, like rabbinical scholars citing the Talmud.

In it we found directions to a *supermarche* in the nearby town of Balin-Mire. In due course I set out, with Lettie as my copilot, green book in hand. Following the directions, we drove out of Savonnieres into the hills surrounding the town, through a countryside where small châteaux, partially hidden from the road, could be seen with occasional low and graceful farmhouses. Donkeys and cattle grazed in their high fields, and forests of poplars and oaks shaded the road.

We entered Balin-Mire on a narrow street and followed it past the church and into the square. The array and amount of flowers was staggering. Everywhere we looked were planters and window boxes and gardens filled with geraniums and impatiens, with colors so bright they seemed unreal. There were huge bushes of apricot and yellow brugmansia, the South American "angel's trumpet," in great containers in the center of town, and even the public buildings—the city hall, the tourist office, the information center—were draped in vivid floral color. Following the excellent directions of my copilot, I drove on until we saw the sign with a large red arrow that read ATAC.

Attack? A perfect name for a supermarket as far as I was concerned. After three decades of shopping professionally, marketing, to me, is like an attack. I have a plan and, like a general in action, know exactly what I need, where it is, and how much I want. Here, in this foreign locality, not being able to speak or read the language, I carefully surveyed the battle site.

Inside I was struck by the absence of fluorescent lights in the produce, meat, fish, and dairy departments. It was, in fact, almost dim. No bright fluorescence sucking the color out of everything. The second thing that caught my eye was the fish counter—a curved, stainless-steel affair about fifteen feet long and about five feet wide, covered with fresh chipped ice and filled with one of the most gratifying arrays of fish I had seen in a long time. So many varieties; some I recognized, a few of the names I could read and understand, yet others completely escaped me. There were three kinds of snails and a great pile of tiny, luminous blue-black mussels. I saw white, skinless eels, fresh tuna and swordfish, eight different kinds of whitefish filleted or steaked out, salmon steaks, and little salmon fillets wrapped around a whitefish mousse. There was squid, octopus, and several varieties of smoked fish. It was so beautifully arranged and looked so fresh you'd swear you could see some of the fish still moving. Unable to resist, I bought a kilo of mussels and mentally began preparing them, ignoring my resolve not to cook for the entire month.

As with the fish, the exhibition of the fruits and vegetables was inspiring. Peaches so mellow you could smell them, strawberries, pears—everything picked and sold at the height of ripeness. Here, apparently, no one was expected, as it was once suggested to me, to take home a pound of stone-hard peaches and put them into a brown paper bag for a couple of days. I tried it once, and what I got was a mealy peach that tasted like a brown paper bag.

The vegetables looked as though they had been picked that morning, all of it elegantly stacked, nothing packaged, everything loose and beautifully arranged. I was having a wonderful time. Lettie had selected some bottles of wine, strawberry jam, and a little package of mousse de canard (duck mousse). When our eyes met across a hill of perfectly ripe avocados and tomatoes, we chuckled.

I was scooping up pleurettes (little French mushrooms) and wonderful green onions that smelled as though they had just come out of the ground as Lettie added a hunk of butter to the cart and went in search of the cheese aisle.

There were *four* aisles of cheeses. Like making your way through the Louvre, you needed more than a single morning to get through it intelligently. Goat cheeses, plain, herbed, or peppered, scores of hard cheeses from France, Italy, and

Switzerland and Germany, numerous varieties of Camemberts, Bries, triple crème Bries, Emmenthals, and roqueforts. The prices ranged from under a dollar for a Brie, to three and four and five dollars for the more special types or brands.

There were sweet cheeses and crèmes fraiches; yogurts; caramel and coffee, vanilla, and fruit-flavored cream custards in little jars, with a half-dozen varieties of each.

At the meat counter there was no "take a number." Everyone simply queued up and politely stood in line waiting their turn. All of the meat—lamb, goat, rabbit, pork, turkey, chicken, horse, sausages, and veal—was cut expressly for each customer. Even the ground beef was ground fresh for each sale. Nothing was prepackaged.

At the far end of the meat counter, Lettie was buying goat cheese (the meat counter had yet another cheese section). After the woman had weighed, wrapped, and priced it, Lettie asked if what she had bought was the most preferred in this region. The woman replied that another was better, and when Lettie requested that instead, she unwrapped the original purchase, then weighed and wrapped the better choice without a sign of impatience.

I had already selected blood sausages and two chickens and was considering rabbits when an employee ran up and said something that ended with the word *fermer*. I knew *fermer* meant they were closing. I looked at the clock—it was noon—and answered back one of the six French words I knew for certain. *"Maintenant?"* (Right now?)

"*Oui, monsieur,*" she replied.

People were hurrying out the doors. Lettie and I headed for the checkout. The young lady sitting at the cash register explained to us we had to weigh the plums ourselves. Grabbing them up, Lettie sprinted back to produce. There were icons instead of numbers on the scale. You simply pressed the corresponding picture and the weight and price were printed out on a little sticker. Rushing back, she grabbed another bottle of wine and a hard Italian cheese, and as soon as *we* bagged our groceries and were checked out, the iron gate slammed behind us. When they say twelve o'clock *ferme*, it's firm.

When we returned and were putting the groceries away, Mona said, "I think I've figured out a way to divide up the expenses. Every time you spend money for something for the house," she continued, "save the receipt, and then once or twice a week we'll bring out the receipts and everyone gets paid back what they spent."

It seemed like a good idea.

"For instance," she went on, "how much did you spend this morning?"

I pulled out two receipts, one for forty-five francs from the patisserie, and another for two hundred and thirty francs from the ATAC.

Using a little calculator she had brought to figure out the exchange rate, Mona quickly totaled them. "That's two hundred and seventy-five francs. Divided by four." She consulted the calculator again. "That's sixty-eight francs, and seventy-five centimes apiece."

Pre-Euro French money is beautiful. It has pictures of poets and writers on the bills and seems, almost, like play money. Mona's plan for calculating the household expenses was a fair and simple system, which we continued to use throughout the month.

~ ~ ~

IT BEING OUR FIRST day in Savonnieres, we were anxious to begin exploring, and after we had returned and put the groceries away, Mona and Jack suggested that we stroll back down into the village for a little lunch. At the far end of town where the bridge crosses the river was La Marina, the last of the three cafés there.

A little plainer looking than the others, even "rugged" judging by the mostly male patrons we saw entering and leaving, it served a daily *plat* between twelve and two as well as the sandwiches the other cafés offered. There was a little garden behind the café with tables (that we didn't discover until later) and more tables around front, across the street beneath the trees, looking out over the wall to the river. We took a seat, and before long, the owner, a burly guy, like a wrestler, came outside and crossed in our direction.

"Uh-oh," Jack said, "this guy looks like trouble."

"Maybe he's going to throw us in the river," I suggested. "Maybe he hates Americans."

Lettie bid him good day and asked if we could get some lunch.

He informed us we could order the plat du jour or a sandwich jambon. The sisters ordered the plat while Jack and I opted for the sandwich jambon (ham sandwich).

The man disappeared back into the café to place our orders, returning a few minutes later with the drinks—a carafe of red wine with two glasses for the ladies, a Coke for me, and a beer for Jack. Solicitous now, he adjusted the umbrella for us, pulled a second table near to our own so there would be more room when the food arrived, and grinned broadly at Lettie.

Within a few minutes, the chef, the owner's wife—a competent-looking and cordial woman—appeared with the tray of food, and dodging traffic, crossed the street to where we sat. The plat turned out to be roast pork with creamed spinach. Sampling a taste from Lettie's dish, I was surprised and impressed with the quality of the food. The sandwich jambon was a slice of lean ham, like prosciutto, on a crusty baguette that had been smeared with butter. Hardly the ham sandwich with lettuce and mayo I had been accustomed to, it was, in fact, as much of a treat as the plat, and from this meal on, the Marina was to become our favorite place for dining out in Savonnieres.

Later that afternoon, we visited a local tourist attraction, les Grottes Petrifiantes de Savonnieres, a series of deep caves discovered in 1547 by a gentleman named Bernard Pallissy. The caves run twelve miles underground and the tour guide informed us they had served as escape routes to local châteaux during the revolution. There were underground lakes—ponds actually; some Gallo-Roman grave sites dating back to the fifth century; and a display titled "an original reconstruction of prehistoric fauna," little stuffed animals that had been placed in the dampness of the calcite falls, where over time they had become encrusted, like fossilized prehistoric beasts. It was a little on the kitschy side, but the caves and the tunnels themselves were impressive, in particular the fifth-century grave sites.

The tour concluded at one of the caves where a little faux café had been set up with a winepress, candles in old wine bottles at the center of the tables, and a long bar where samples of local white, red, and rosé wines, pressed and aged in the caves, were being offered to taste.

The crowd was of mixed nationalities—some French, some German, some Spanish, and, of course, us. As everyone was enjoying the wine, I stepped back from the crowd and, opening my camera, announced loudly, *"Pardonnez-moi, mesdames et messieurs,"* motioning for everyone to squeeze together for a photograph. Completely mortified, my companions joined the crowd, which happily obeyed.

"Say *fromage*," I directed.

Looking at each other, and wondering, I suppose, why they were being asked to say fromage, everyone complied, and I snapped the picture.

"Well, fine," Mona complained in mock embarrassment,

after the group had dispersed, "now I can never come here again."

From the caves we drove on to the château at Villandry, less than a mile down the road. Erected in the sixteenth century, the house was purchased in the latter part of the nineteenth century by an American heiress, Ann Coleman, and her Spanish husband, Joachim Carvallo. It was he who had the obliterated moats redug and who razed the English park that surrounded the house to establish the famous gardens seen there today: an historical interpretation in the style of the era from which the château dates.

Constructed on three levels with surrounding elevations for viewing the beautiful patterns of its intricate boxwood parterres, this tour de force with its flowers, fountains and canals, moats and mazes, and especially its elaborate *potagers* (vegetable gardens) bordered with hedges of foot-high espaliered apple trees, is truly remarkable. The lavender was at its peak, with roses, dahlias and petunias, impatiens and zinnias providing a vibrant mix of color accenting the lustrous green of the boxwood. We spent the better part of three hours touring this splendid garden and still felt unable to take it all in. Stopping for a drink at the little café outside its gates, we considered our good fortune to have discovered ourselves living so close to this remarkable place which we felt certain we would visit again.

≈ ≈ ≈

LATER THAT AFTERNOON, MARIE-CLAIRE appeared at the house to show us how to run the washer and dryer. The laundry was located at the far end of the house in a little dirt-floored milk room. The last time I had traveled in Europe, one of the most vexing problems had been finding a place to do laundry, so I was particularly grateful for this amenity.

On her way out she stopped and, narrowing her eyes, shook a finger at us in a gesture of great seriousness, cautioning us to "always lock the house and the gate ... Gypsies! ... even when you are home, or you will find the furniture gone!"

Gypsies? Seeing her to the gate, I checked twice to see if I had secured it correctly and wondered, Would they have time to read my fortune while carrying out the sofa?

Dinner

Steamed Mussels in White Wine, Garlic, and Butter
Blood Sausages Fried with New Potatoes and Rosemary in Olive
  Oil
Sautéed Green Beans
Apple-and-Pear Tart in a Butter Pastry
Cuvée des Grottes Petrifiantes Rouge

THAT EVENING I STEAMED the mussels in a couple cups of inexpensive dry white wine, about four tablespoons of chopped garlic, and a half cup of butter. While they were steaming I fried up the blood sausages with thin-sliced potatoes in a little olive oil and butter, fresh rosemary from the garden, and some salt and pepper. Lettie picked several handfuls of green beans, which I sautéed in olive oil with garlic, salt, and pepper. I was having a wonderful time in the kitchen!

We drank Badouit, a local mineral water, and a bottle of the Cuvée des Grottes Petrifiantes Rouge we had bought at the caves. For dessert I baked an apple-and-pear tart.

To make the crust I put what I hoped was a half pound of butter (since the butter didn't come cut into quarters, I had to eyeball a half pound), two cups of flour, one egg, and three tablespoons of ice water into the food processor and, with the blade, pulsed it until it seemed completely mixed.

I usually make this "pastry" with a pound of butter, one egg, seven tablespoons of ice water, and four and a quarter cups of flour. It's a never-fail recipe. But this time, since I was making only half the quantity and was not certain of the amount of butter, the pastry dough never formed a ball, becoming instead somewhat mushy in consistency. By continuously dipping my fingers in soft butter to keep them from sticking to the dough, I pushed it around until it filled the plate. I peeled, cored, and sliced two apples and two pears and laid them on the dough in concentric circles. I sprinkled the fruit with a half cup of sugar, a dash of cinnamon, and a great hunk of butter and baked it at 350 degrees F. for about an hour until the fruit was a caramelized brown. The crust cooked up like a puff pastry, glistening and golden on the edges. We devoured the entire dish and spent the rest of the evening sitting on the terrace finishing off another bottle of wine and watching the sky turn violet and orange with the setting sun.

Saturday, July 18

THE NEXT MORNING I came downstairs before any of the others were up and set the table with blue-and-white Limoges. I put on the coffee and walked down to the local patisserie to fetch apple, chocolate, and almond croissants and a baguette. On returning, I put some music on the tape machine and settled myself on the terrace with a cup of that strong French coffee.

The morning couldn't have been more perfect: warm but not hot, with a low dew point. Bees worked their way from flower to flower. A pair of doves and other small birds flew among the branches of the peach trees in the garden. It felt as if THE END had just come up on the movie screen and now the part where they all lived happily ever after was beginning. Sipping the strong black coffee, I knew I'd never be able to drink weak coffee again.

The flirtation with France had evolved into love's first kiss.

~ ~ ~

LETTIE PUSHED OPEN THE window from her bathroom and leaned on the sill, the pink-apricot roses framing her silver hair. Smiling a broad grin, she greeted me.

"Bonjour, monsieur."

"Ah, bonjour, madame," I replied. We were like children playing "pretend."

The day had begun. We indulged ourselves with the fresh, buttery, and flaky croissants filled with *amandes, pommes,* and *chocolat.* The baguette, still warm from the oven, had a paper-thin crust, shiny and toasty in color, the bread beneath it light and coarse. We blanketed it with that incredibly delicious French butter.

It was Saturday. The "green book" informed us that "les Halles," the food market in the nearby city of Tours, would be open and we decided to make this excursion. After breakfast, we piled into the car. Lettie sat in the front, green book in hand, relating the directions to me as I drove, and Jack and Mona sat in the back. Between the green book, the road signs, and of course the guidance from the ladies, we were soon in Tours.

We inquired for directions from a passerby and headed for

the market. A large yellow sign with black letters on the front of a building we passed en route advertising ANTIQUITÉS drew our attention. Looking through the windows of the shop, Lettie spotted some copper pots hanging from the ceiling, and we went inside. After the courtesies of the day, Lettie inquired about the pots and the old woman who owned the shop dragged a tall stepladder out of the corner, climbed up, and brought one down. Lettie and Mona examined the pot carefully then asked to see another and then another. Dutifully the old woman politely dragged the ladder along, clambering up and down each time.

While this transaction was going on I examined a set of four simple, pale gray dishes with hand-painted striping in blue, and two little soup dishes, the same color gray but with a garland of hand-painted flowers encircling the bottom of each dish. Not fine china, but rustic, everyday plates. I was tempted to buy them, but decided to wait with the thought that perhaps I might find something even better somewhere else in the weeks ahead. Realizing the market would soon close for that two-hour lunch, Lettie left a down payment on the pots and made arrangements to pick them up another day.

≈ ≈ ≈

LES HALLES IS AN enclosed central marketplace and has been there for centuries. The building itself is not old; in fact, it looks out of place among the eighteenth- and nineteenth-century neighborhoods that surround it. I was a bit disappointed in the block-long white-metal-and-brick edifice; it lacked the distinction I was expecting. But once I was inside, my spirits lifted. Not unlike the ATAC, the French had somehow taken the modern idea of supermarket and were able to incorporate the traditions of their culture without losing any of the sense or quality of the past.

There was a seemingly endless variety of pastries, tarts, croissants, rolls and breads, cakes and desserts, all of it carefully and meticulously arranged and beautifully decorated. Again I noticed the absence of bright or fluorescent lights.

From the fruit section we could smell the strawberries as we approached. Perfect in size, each finger-shaped berry red and ripe, ready to eat at that moment. We bought a quart to take home. Mona pointed out the strangest peaches any of us had ever seen: little, flat fruit, a deep russet color. We bought four to taste. The flesh inside was white, sweet, and juicy. As we wolfed them down we agreed that this was the ultimate peach. We bought a dozen more to take with us.

At the dairy counter, we agreed on a selection of three cheeses: a soft Italian, a creamy Camembert, and a local goat cheese. Lettie requested half a kilo from an enormous mound of fresh butter, and the man behind the counter lopped off a great chunk, wrapped it up, and handed it to her as she passed him a handful of francs.

Moving on to the fish section, I picked out a few pieces of mixed and boned-out whitefish. Once again, unable to recognize the names, I simply pointed, requesting, *"S'il vous plaît."* At a stall filled with delicacies from the Mideast, we bought huge flat white haricot beans called *soissons*, a pint of hot and spicy Moroccan olives, and some green peppercorns. Just to walk through this market was a treat. To see and taste and smell all of this wonderful food was so heartening to me, I felt I had arrived in heaven.

By noon, people began closing down for lunch. We headed across the street to a small sidewalk café and sat down. Mona, Lettie, and I ordered a tomato salad with fresh mozzarella and basil, but Jack opted for "le cheval burger avec frites," a hamburger made from horse meat with french fries.

"How can you eat that?" Mona asked. "Don't you feel like you're eating a pet?"

"Not at all," he replied. "If you're willing to eat a piece of cow, what's the logic at drawing the line at horse? Want a bite?" he asked, offering her the sandwich.

Grimacing, she put up a hand to fend it off.

"Could you eat horse meat?" Lettie asked me.

"I'm a cook," I replied confidently. "I eat everything."

"Except eel," Jack reminded me.

"Except eel," I agreed emphatically.

~ ~ ~

ON THE GREEN, ACROSS from us, farmers sat leaning against their trucks, legs stretched out on the grass, eating cheese and bread, breaking open melons, and sharing bottles of wine. It was a scene that must have been replayed for centuries by their fathers, grandfathers, and great-grandfathers. It lacked a sense of urgency. No one was checking their watches or leaping up to get back to work. Instead, they joked good-naturedly back and forth, enjoyed another glass of wine, lit up a Galoise or a Gitane, and continued to relax. It all seemed so civilized.

Lunch over, we headed for the car, loaded down with our provisions. The return was not as easy as the coming. First we had some difficulty relocating the car, then, since we had driven around and around so many times looking for a parking place, we somehow lost track of the main street and the way out of Tours. I stopped for directions several times, but in French they were confusing even to Lettie. We asked a passing couple for directions, which Lettie and Mona were able to translate for me, and much to my surprise we found our way back on Winston Churchill Boulevard—the same road we had taken that first day from the train station. I knew where we were from there.

As soon as we were home, I unpacked the groceries. I was beginning dinner when the bell clanged and we heard the gate opening. We looked at each other in alarm. Someone had forgotten to lock the gate!

"Oh God . . . Gypsies!" Mona exclaimed, remembering Marie-Claire's warning.

Instinctively, Lettie grabbed her purse and clutched it to herself yelling, "Tell them we don't need anything . . . Don't let them near the house."

"Is the car locked?" Jack asked with an air that lacked seriousness.

Prepared for the worst, the four of us rushed out onto the terrace. Where were the gendarmes when you needed them? I wondered. But instead of a band of marauding Gypsies, a short man in a comical straw hat, white T-shirt, plaid shorts, and a pair of well-worn sneakers greeted us, smiling broadly. *"Bonjour! Bienvenue!"*

It was Monsieur Dumont, the handyman.

We offered him a glass of wine, he toasted our health and, delighted to discover Lettie spoke French, conversed happily with us in a combination of his own broken English and her translations while I continued making the dinner.

Dinner

Chowder Français with Croutons Provençal
Strawberries with Crème Fraîche
Chilled Vouvray

I WARMED AND THEN strained the juices left from last night's steamed mussels through a coffee filter (to remove any possi-

ble grit from the shells) into a soup pot. Then I added the leftover ratatouille from the charcuterie, about two cups each of
cut-up potatoes and onions, some garlic, salt, pepper, and butter, two cups of white wine and a cup of water, and brought it
all to a rolling boil. After the potatoes had cooked to softness,
I turned down the heat and added a little flour mixed in white
wine for thickening, the whitefish from the market, and
enough milk to cover, and simmered it until the fish began to
break apart.

Leaning over the stove in appreciation of the scent of the
soup, Monsieur Dumont asked who was doing all the cooking. When Lettie told him it was me, he shrugged in an atti-
tude of sympathy and as a parting gesture pronounced in
French, "Ah, men are always the martyrs." What man could
disagree? He announced he would be leaving in the morning
for a short vacation but would return in ten days and be
available should we need him.

After he had gone, I cut the leftover baguettes from the
morning into rounds, spread butter and garlic over them, and
broiled them until they toasted. We drank a bottle of Vouvray with dinner, and for dessert ate almost a quart of the
strawberries covered with crème fraîche and a little sugar,
marveling at how perfectly wonderful even the most simple
food tasted when you were eating it in France.

Breakfast

Peach Crepes with Homemade Strawberry Sauce

JUST BEFORE SEVEN, MADELINE called to say that she and Helmut, due to arrive in Paris that morning, were *still* at Logan Airport. Their flight had been delayed twice because of mechanical failures, and now, already seven hours late, they were waiting on a third plane and would call as soon as they got to France. Mona relayed the tale of their travail: sleeping on the floor of the terminal, nothing open, no coffee, no sandwiches, no blankets, and no one from the airlines offering any explanations, let alone an apology.

We urged her to tell them the house would transform all that, that being here would make their suffering worthwhile.

After they had hung up, we, of course, continued to discuss their dilemma.

"According to Madeline," Mona said, "Helmut was just about at the edge."

"I hope they don't change their minds," Jack said.

"They wouldn't change their minds and not come at all, would they?" I worried.

"I don't know," Mona replied. "We'll just have to wait and see . . ."

≈ ≈ ≈

SINCE WE WERE ALL up, Lettie offered to make peach crepes. Whipping up the batter, she related this story.

"Every now and again I try to do something different for the kids in my class. You know, bring in some music or some photos of Europe," she began, pitting four of the little white-flesh peaches and dicing them into a bowl. "So this one morning I decided I was going to make crepes for them. Getting a gas burner into the classroom was no easy task," she continued, mixing in three-quarters of a cup of flour, two eggs, and a cup of water. "They all seemed very interested watching me make the batter. I poured it into the pan and began working it from side to side . . ."

Lettie mashed the last of the strawberries into a pan with a couple tablespoons of water and a tablespoon of sugar to make a little sauce for the crepes. "I explained that these were *crêpes*—French pancakes—and when the first one was done, I took it out of the pan, rolled it up with some jam, cut it into pieces, and asked, 'Who wants to try the first piece?' Well, nobody moved."

Watching as she poured the batter into the pan and began working it from side to side, we waited, hungry for both the crepes and the story.

"I was crushed. Here I had gone to all this trouble getting the darn gas burner, bringing in all the makings, and now the little stinkers refused to eat them."

She flipped the first crepe over.

"I offered it again and again, but no one moved, so I asked, 'For heaven's sake, why don't you want to at least try them?' And you know what they said?"

She plunked a crepe down on Jack's dish as we sat waiting expectantly for the answer.

"They said because they weren't *round*!"

Confused, I asked, "Weren't round?"

"Yes, weren't round, like their mothers made," Lettie explained, pouring more batter into the pan. "They were talking about the kind you put into a toaster, the round frozen pancakes!"

I don't know about those students, but we found the peach crepes, though slightly lopsided, to be a triumph.

———

≈ ≈ ≈

LATER THAT MORNING THE four of us decided to take a walk out to the sunflower fields we could see from our bedroom windows. The road wound out along the river, through the empty fairgrounds, and past a collection of farm buildings. Four-foot-high bushes of lavender and spikes of pink hollyhocks leaned against antique stone walls, and purple hydrangea languished over moss-covered steps the present inhabitants hadn't used in years. Beyond and into the heart of the fields, with giant rolls of hay resplendent in the sun on one side, sunflowers on the other, it was like stumbling into a van Gogh painting.

I don't think I have seen quite as peaceful a place as this—ever. I don't know what I expected, but this was a feeling I hadn't anticipated.

Sunflowers, where I grew up and even where I live now, were something you'd see from time to time by the side of someone's house, or a few stalks at the end of a garden. But here! Here you could stroll through them for an hour and still not be home.

Everywhere I looked was beauty—the fields, the houses, the gardens. This incredible elegance survived centuries of invaders, first with crossbow then with tank, and still, after it all, had endured and continued to flourish.

The walk into the fields of sunflowers and rolled hay bales became a daily routine for me. Farm dogs came out to bark as

I passed, but after the third or fourth day, they began to recognize me and only came out to look and then return to the shade.

Lunch

Moroccan Olive Salad

THAT AFTERNOON WE SAT on the terrace in the bright Touraine sun enjoying a simple salad of rocket lettuce, the Moroccan olives, a few tomatoes, and four hard-boiled eggs, with a semisoft cheese grated over the top. Lettie mixed up a dressing with the juice of two lemons, about half a cup of olive oil, a couple of smashed garlic cloves, some salt, pepper, and a bunch of fresh basil leaves. We sipped white wine and ate strawberries. Mona had spent the morning painting in the garden. Wearing a wraparound and a straw hat, she was beginning to look like a painting herself.

We continued to be concerned about Madeline and Helmut.

By three that afternoon they called from Paris to say the plane, though nine hours late, had finally arrived and they would be on the six-thirty train that evening at St.-Pierre-des-Corps. You could tell from Madeline's voice that everything was not perfect.

"Wait till you get here," Mona promised encouragingly. "Just wait till you see the house."

~ ~ ~

IN THE SHORT SPACE between Wednesday and Sunday, the four of us had become a tight, happy, and resourceful unit. While we eagerly awaited the arrival of our friends, we also felt a certain apprehension. Though we had shared a number of pleasurable dinners, none of us had ever lived together, and this present mix had turned out so well that we worried the newcomers' disgruntled state of mind would affect the completely carefree feeling the four of us had created these first couple of days.

By six o'clock, Jack and I had left for the station at St.-Pierre-des-Corps.

Madeline saw us first and called out, "Jack! Buddy! Here we are." Exhausted, they dragged their bags to the car as we ran to help them.

Happy and cheerful, I was even annoyingly perky as we loaded their suitcases into the trunk.

"Well, you two look great. I think a night on the floor of Logan Airport did wonders for the both of you."

Madeline looked me square in the eye and stuck out her tongue. She and Jack got into the backseat and Helmut, who stands well over six feet, wedged himself into the front.

"If it seems a little cramped, you can hang one leg out the window," I suggested as I started the car.

"I'll be fine." It was the first words he had spoken to us.

Crossing the bridge onto Winston Churchill Boulevard, I began a commentary mimicking a tour guide, not quite Pa Kettle, not exactly Mr. Chips.

"There's the mall and a Toys 'Я' Us . . . that's a water tower." I could have just as easily been describing Dover, New Hampshire. "Over there, but you can't see it from here, the river, well, it's over there someplace." Neither one of them seemed amused.

Jack inquired about the trip. "Agghh," Madeline began, still exasperated by the galling indifference of the airline to their comfort. "After all of the ineptitude at Logan, when we finally got on the plane, the *third* one they brought, and nine hours late, mind you, the pilot comes out of the cockpit and matter-of-factly tells us, 'Look, I'm only the pilot. If you have any complaints call this number,' and then he gives us a phone number. A phone number! Not even an apology!"

Helmut's face was expressionless, but he began to recover a little bit, taking an interest as, spinning through the traffic circle, crossing the bridge over the River Cher, I hung a right on route D-7 with as much ease as if I had been doing it all my life.

"You really know your way around here. I'm impressed," he said, breaking his silence. Coming from the owner of a professional driving service, the compliment was appreciated that much more.

We had left the busy city boulevard behind and were heading into the evening light that reflected the color of hay fields. Madeline and Helmut slowly began to relax. Everything was being taken care of from here on out.

On the outskirts of Savonnieres, I pulled off the main road onto Rue de la Liberté a few blocks from our house. At a rundown, barnlike building with broken machinery in the yard, I slowed the car to a near stop as though I was about to park. "This is it!" I said with great enthusiasm. "Well, what do you think?"

Expressionless once again, Helmut sat silently. Madeline muttered an unenthusiastic "ahh."

"Only kidding," I said, continuing up the road. No one laughed at the joke. A moment later I stopped in front of the maison, honked the horn, and Mona opened the gates. We drove up the drive and parked in front of the terrace steps. Lettie came out to greet the new arrivals.

It was as if whatever aggravations they had endured in their long ordeal had been left outside when we closed and locked the gates. Proudly we led our friends on a tour through the house and garden. Their reactions were the same as ours had been that first day.

While they showered, Lettie and Mona set the table for dinner with the blue-and-white Limoges and Jack picked a bouquet of flowers for the center. Refreshed and serene, the newcomers joined us on the terrace, where we shared a bottle of wine. Helmut's face relaxed into a wide smile as he and Madeline recounted the trials of their money-saving charter. Even they were able to somehow find the humor as we alternately gasped then roared at the telling of every indignity.

Dinner

Cassoulet with Sausage and Soissons
Vanilla Apple Tart

I WANTED THE FOOD their first night to reflect as much of France as could be put onto a plate. A "cassoulet," or my version thereof, a dish more native to Provence than here, seemed perfect. The wide flat beans (*soissons*) had been soaked overnight, then boiled until they were soft. I saved the water they were cooked in, adding a couple of cups of white wine, a few cut-up potatoes, six links of herbed sausage (cut into bite-size pieces), five or six carrots, some small green onions from the garden, a generous amount of garlic, a handful of fresh rosemary and thyme, a quarter cup of tomato paste, and salt and pepper. I put it into a hot oven at about 450 degrees F. for fifteen to twenty minutes to let it brown up, stirred it, then covered it and turned the oven down to 350, letting it cook for an hour. I served the cassoulet with baguettes and tons of butter and, for dessert, another apple tart, this time flavored with pure vanilla.

Helmut had barely shoveled in the last bite of tart when he said, "I'm sorry, folks, but I've had it. I've got to sleep."

"Me, too," Madeline agreed. "Wake me in two days."

Hugging us all good night, exhausted, they headed for their bedroom.

Breakfast

Pleurette Omelet

Toasted Baguette with Emmenthal

THERE WERE A HANDFUL of pleurettes (little mushrooms) left from a day before, and having walked down to the patisserie for a couple of baguettes, I hurried back to the kitchen to make a mushroom omelet for the others who were not yet up.

I chopped a green onion and a couple of shallots into the pan with two tablespoons of olive oil and a hunk of butter, simmered them until they had become soft, added the pluerettes, and sautéed them until they had begun to brown. Whipping together a dozen eggs with the last of the crème fraîche (about a cup and a half) and a little salt and pepper and fresh basil, I poured it over the pleurettes and onions, then covered the pan, turned the heat very low, and let it cook for about fifteen minutes. While the omelet was cooking I cut the baguettes lengthwise, covered them with slices of Emmenthal, and put them under the broiler until they toasted up bubbly and the edges of the bread and cheese became crispy.

By nine o'clock, Madeline and Helmut appeared at the table, completely rested, ravenously hungry, and very anxious to see the countryside.

After breakfast, we drove into Balin-Mire, where we had found a patisserie that had the most exceptional stock of dulcet delicacies I had ever seen. The array of confections, breads, pastries, and candies was a feast. There were long, shiny baguettes, crusty round pain de compagnes, oblong loaves, thick-crusted wheat breads, and rolls baked together on a long loaf glistening like toasty leaves. In the cold case were brightly decorated chocolate and lemon mousse cakes covered with a raspberry gelatin. There were patisserie crème-stuffed éclairs, napoleons, and cocoa-dusted edible boxes filled with chocolate mousse like we had eaten our first night in Savonnieres. There were trays of confections that looked more like edible toys than pastries: little meringues in the shape of mice and swans dipped in chocolate; whipped-cream cakes and fruit tarts covered with strawberries and kiwis, peaches and apples, or a beautiful and colorful mix of four fruits all masterfully decorated.

My mother, who is eighty-two years old and has been widowed for three years, lives alone in a small town in Illinois. Before we left for France I had called to ask what I could send her. "Oh, something to eat!" she replied quickly. "But don't forget, I'm not supposed to have anything with nuts in it anymore."

The saleslady offered a cordial *"Bonjour, monsieur"* and (probably) asked what she could help me with. Struggling with my French, I tried to explain what I wanted. "A box of candies to send to my mother. No nuts, please."

"Ahh, oui, monsieur."

I picked out the box I wanted—it had pictures of the châteaux on it—and the saleslady began pointing out the selections. *"Café? Crème au chocolat? Framboisse? Aux fraises?"* she asked courteously, adding to the little box, a few chocolates at a time, as I nodded an approval at each singling out.

In the short time since we had been talking, the shop, which had been empty when we arrived, began filling up with patrons. If they were becoming impatient, there was no sign of it. As I selected the different candies, I could not help but think of my mother's advanced age and the realization that time was now closing in on her. Images of her from other, younger times, suddenly filled my thoughts, and between the selections of butter creams and coconut creams, and unnoticed in the middle of all the beautiful cakes and tarts and pastries, I could feel my face begin to flush and my eyes well up with tears.

The saleslady finished packing up the little box. *"Paquet cadeau?"* she asked, meaning did I want her to gift-wrap the box. *"Par courrier?"* By mail?

"Oui, madame," I replied, deflecting my eyes to hide the sadness. She began to double-wrap the box for mailing, first in a bright green cellophane tied with a pink ribbon, then into another box, tied with yet another ribbon. I thanked her, uttered a *"Merci, mesdames et messieurs,"* to the other patrons for their patience, and left to wait outside for my companions.

A church stood just across from the patisserie. With my little package of candy in hand, I went in and sat down in one of the pews. A recording of a Bach cantata filled the space and soft light streamed through the ancient stained-glass windows. I thought about how much my mother would have loved the food in France and how, when I was a little boy, she would buy me a dime's worth of cheese or smoked fish when we went shopping just so I could taste it. It was through her that I had acquired my appreciation of food.

The others soon found me and we quietly walked through the old building, examining every dark corner, admiring the statues and paintings. As we were leaving, Lettie discovered a message board filled with handwritten notes to loved ones who had passed away. Our attention was caught by a note from a little boy to his grandfather which said (in French), "Dear Grandpapa, I miss you every day and wish you were still here. I know that you and everyone in heaven would be happy to know that France has won the Coupe du Monde. Please say hello to God for me."

While I was immersed in my childhood reminiscences inside the church, my friends had purchased seven eclairs, three chocolate and four coffeee. We shared them convivally in the car on the way back.

≈ ≈ ≈

OUR FEARS THAT THE new arrivals might alter the mix that had been so harmonious proved unfounded. The comfortable old house was able to accommodate the increase with ease, and Helmut and Madeline were a sweet-tempered addition. I was particularly delighted to find Helmut anxious to take over the driving. Getting the (not so) large four-seater car to accommodate all six of us took some doing. With a little practice we quickly mastered the trick of maneuvering ourselves into the small car, two in the front, usually Helmut and Lettie (he drove, she asked directions), and the rest of us jammed in the back. Since Helmut was so tall, he had to push his seat back as far as it could go to give him room to use the gas and brake pedals. Instead of room for just two in the back, this now left room for about one and a half people. We were hardly the nineteen-year-olds you might expect to see cramming themselves into so tiny a space. It was a comic sight to see six middle-aged adults, emerging from a restaurant perhaps, casually walking toward the car, reasonably respectable and sober looking, and then, as if a lever had been pulled, piling into the little car like the reverse of the circus act where fifteen midgets come pouring out of a Volkswagen. Even the natives, hard-pressed to crack a smile, would break into a laugh when viewing our auto antics.

≈ ≈ ≈

THAT AFTERNOON I WALKED over to the post office to mail the candy home. The postmistress smiled from behind the window at me.

"*Bonjour, monsieur.*"

"*Bonjour, madame,*" I replied, pushing the box through to her. "*Par avion, si'l vous plaît. Aux U.S.A.*"

"*Ah, oui, monsieur,*" she answered.

I was delighted with myself that I had spoken a sentence, more or less, and had actually been understood.

Pushing a lengthy questionnaire back through the window, she rattled off an entire paragraph that I did not understand. Completely in the dark, I stared blankly at her for a few moments then broke into an embarrassed laugh. She joined in. A second lady came in from the back, said something to the postmistress, who answered her, and she joined in the laughter. Eventually they were able to help me understand that I had not only to fill out the address but list the contents as well.

"*Des chocolats pour ma mere,*" I offered.

"Ahh." Immediately her tone became very respectful. "*Pour votre mere. C'est bon.*"

When we had completed the questionnaire, she attached a "par avion" sticker and a colorful collection of stamps, and announced, *"Voilà."*

Thinking it might be a good idea to add a red "fragile" sticker, I inquired, *"Possible . . . marquer marchandise fragile?"*

"Oh, non, non, non!" she answered emphatically. Clearly aghast at the suggestion, she stretched her arms over her head as though she were holding a large package and began to shake it violently back and forth, announcing, *"Marchandise fragile!"*

There are some aspects of all cultures that are exactly alike.

≈ ≈ ≈

LUNCH THAT DAY WAS a casual affair. We sat on the terrace and ate fruit and cheese and sipped wine. For dessert we ate petit suisse. Petit suisse comes in a cylindrically shaped plastic container and tastes like a cross between yogurt and crème fraîche. The trick is to make a small hole in the bottom, then turn the container over and tap it so that the petit suisse slips out in one piece. With a sprinkle of sugar over the top, it becomes a sweet little dessert. We had lots of petits suisses in the refrigerator. Lettie was crazy for it. Every time we went shopping she would remind us, "Don't forget the petits suisses." In fact, at one time we had amassed more than three dozen containers.

We also had lots of little jars of different-flavored custards: crème caramel, crème vanille, and café crème. Mona had taken to saving the little containers that were just slightly smaller then baby-food jars and shaped like miniature vases. At one point the entire kitchen window counter was filled with them, all washed and neatly aligned.

"What are you going to do with them?" I interrogated.

Mona replied that she wasn't certain but declared, "Aren't they great!"

They *were* great. We used them for little vases for flower arrangements and Mona and Lettie both used them for their watercolors, capping them up and taking them with them wherever they went to paint.

As I sat on the terrace that afternoon, drinking lemon soda and watching Lettie cutting flowers in the garden, I thought about the age of the town and tried to imagine what it might have been like in the first century when the Romans arrived. Did they stand in this spot where the house is? Had they built fires, cooked, and washed clothes here in the garden? In nineteen hundred years, thousands of people must have walked in this place.

The present owner, who, with her husband, had so attentively restored the house and garden, was now widowed. Her husband had not lived long enough to realize their dream of retiring here. Yet I had the distinct feeling that the spirit of his pleasure had since taken up residence. The garden felt buoyant and rich. Now we were adding our presence to this history. I lifted my glass in solidarity. Lettie cut roses from the trellis, put them into a vase, and placed them next to the door on a white marble tabletop.

Dinner

Roast Chicken Stuffed with Cassoulet
Apricot Lavender Tart

FOR DINNER I HAD bought three chickens for roasting. I made a stuffing from the leftover cassoulet mixed with the heels of the toasted cheese baguettes from breakfast, a few chopped scallions, a handful of herbes de Provence (a mixture of thyme, rosemary, marjoram, savory, and basil), and about a cup each of melted butter, chopped celery, white wine, and one egg. I rubbed the chickens down with garlic and olive oil, salt-and-peppered them inside and out, stuffed them, and baked them uncovered for about fifteen minutes at 450 degrees F. Then I poured about an inch of white wine into the bottom of the pan, covered the birds, turned the heat down to 350, and let them cook until they were tender to the poke of a fork (about forty-five minutes to an hour). With them I served fresh green beans out of the garden, which I had simply sautéed in garlic and olive oil.

For dessert I lined one of the tart pans with a round of puff pastry I had discovered for sale at the ATAC. (A round of pre-made puff pastry! Unless you're a cook you will never understand what a great convenience this is. I bought three packages.) I put in halved apricots with a sliced apple in the center (since I didn't have enough apricots), poured one cup of sugar mixed with six eggs and a little vanilla over the fruit, and across the top laid three perfect strands of lavender. I baked the dish on a low heat, 325 degrees F. for about an hour. The eggs combined with the juice from the apricots and formed a custard gently flavored with the lavender. A very remarkable combination, I thought.

As we were about to sit down to dinner, Marie-Claire came by to drop off a second set of keys. She seemed appreciative of the chickens but was horrified when I pointed out the apricot-lavender tart; she insisted that we should not be eating flowers. "It is not healthy." With the final admonition—"*ne mangez pas les fleurs!*"—she bid us "*bonsoir*" and, shaking her head from side to side in disbelief, left to prepare supper for her own family. No flowers, I'm sure.

The chickens were wonderful and the apricot-lavender tart was devoured notwithstanding the warnings from Marie-Claire.

≈ ≈ ≈

After dinner, the six of us walked the Rue de la Liberté out of the village to the top of the ridge, where there was a beautiful view of the valley. At nine o'clock the light was bright still, golden across the already yellow fields of straw and sun-flowers. As we stood there enjoying the scene beneath us, a couple waved from their garden and invited us to come and drink a lemonade with them.

They spoke a halting but proficient English and introduced themselves as Abelard and Simone. We introduced ourselves and explained where we were staying in the village.

"How long are you staying?" Simone inquired. In her late thirties, she was slender and very pretty, with dark hair that hung in a loosely tied ponytail.

"For a month," Lettie told her.

"You are, uh . . ." Abelard paused, groping momentarily for the correct word. "Married?" he asked, indicating Mona and myself. We laughed, shaking our heads definitively no. Mona explained that her husband and son would be arriving in two weeks.

They called to their daughters, Sabine and Monique, to meet us. Like teenagers everywhere, the girls came out, saw we were "old people," respectfully said hello, then returned to whatever they were doing. We thought it unfortunate that Rory was not there.

"My son is fourteen," Mona told them. "About your daughters' age."

The couple nodded sympathetically.

We spent a pleasant hour visiting and invited them to come by late afternoon on Wednesday. By this time the sky had grown overcast and a steady wind had begun to blow.

Abelard told us that the road continued past their house and circled back into the center of Savonnieres. He also warned us that this was a region of severe storms. Bidding our new friends farewell, we started off. We had gone perhaps half a mile when the sky completely darkened and the wind accelerated to an almost galelike force, blowing errant strands of straw and dried corn leaves onto our paths. Lettie, Mona, and I were concerned that we wouldn't make it home before the rains fell, but Helmut, Madeline, and Jack fairly danced along the road, enjoying this dramatic break from the utterly perfect weather we had been forced to "endure" since our arrival.

Within half an hour we were back in Savonnieres and still the rains had not come. We rushed through the house, closing and bolting windows from the weather. Marie-Claire called to warn us we should move the car back from the cliffs because the storm could send dirt and rocks crashing down onto it.

Exhilarated from the walk, the weather, and our new friends, we sat down to a late snack of petit suisse, a little wine, and a couple of chocolate bars. The winds howled and the rains teased, but the great storm never came.

Tuesday, July 21

IT HAD BECOME MY habit to get up early, put on the coffee, set the plank table, and then hurry down the street for baguettes and croissants. I felt like a cross between a friar and my grandmother.

At the patisserie, I bought almond croissants, little apple tarts, and pain au chocolat. Chocolate bread is a wonderful treat. It's a buttery and flaky croissant filled with pieces of chocolate—not chocolate chips, but chocolate pieces. Once, years before, on a train leaving Paris, I saw a couple of twelve- or thirteen-year-old kids get on, each carrying a baguette. They ripped the loaves open lengthwise and proceeded to glee-fully stuff them with large chocolate bars and gorge them-selves with the treat. I could only imagine their mother handing them a few francs, dutifully saying, "Make sure you eat something on the train."

I certainly was not twelve years old, but I had the same gleeful feeling as I unwrapped the pain au chocolat that morning.

After I had arranged the pastries on a platter, I put music on the tape machine and settled into a chair on the terrace with a cup of strong black coffee, and quietly sat there, feeling content.

≈ ≈ ≈

I WAS DETERMINED TO keep up my regime of working out while I was in France and the green book had indicated an "athletic club" could be found in Balin-Mire. Later that morning I drove off with Lettie, Mona, and Madeline, who wanted to do some shopping, to find the health club. Spotting a sign with an arrow and the word GYM on the outside wall of a house, we parked the car.

The gate was unlocked. Inside there was a small vegetable garden and a neatly trimmed lawn. Elegant, white lace half curtains hung from the windows. I knocked on the door. An old—I mean old—gentleman came out, looked me up and down, and said something in French.

This can't possibly be the gym, I thought. This guy certainly isn't working out. He can barely walk, let alone get on a treadmill. "S'il vous plaît, la gym?" I asked. The old man stared blankly at me. Again I asked, *"...uh...la gym?"* Looking me up and down again, he closed the door, disappearing back into the house. Stymied, I stood there akwardly for a moment. Just as I was turning to descend the steps, an elderly woman (presumably his wife), in a blue dress with matching blue shoes, opened the door.

"Oui, monsieur?" she asked.

Once again I pursued, *"Ah, s'il vous plaît, la gym?"* She seemed bewildered by the question. I turned to my friends, who were waiting at the garden gate. "You've got to help me here," I called to them.

Lettie came up the walk, followed by Madeline and Mona, and explained to the woman that I was looking for the gym. Somewhat surprised, she replied that it was just around the corner, but there were no games today. *"Pas de football,"* she said, using the French word for "soccer."

"There are no soccer games today," Mona interpreted.

I began to mime lifting weights. *"Oh...la musculation!"* the woman said, at last understanding my inquiries, breaking into a wide grin. Pointing toward the road out of town, she began giving what I assumed to be lengthy directions, in the middle of which, Lettie beaming, turned and said, "She just told me I had beautiful teeth."

"Congratulations," I replied, "so how do we get to the gym?" By now my three companions were looking down at the woman's feet, talking excitedly.

"Did you get the directions?" I asked again.

"We were telling her what lovely shoes she has," Mona announced. "She's telling us how to find the store in Tours where she bought them."

How an inquiry for the directions to the gym ended up in a discussion on open-toed wedgies is beyond me. Had the old man been able to understand what I was asking, I'm certain he would have simply given me directions and I would have been on my way without a word about his shoes. Eventually we found the *place de musculation* and I signed up.

On the way home, we stopped for lunch at a little café north of Savonnieres. We sat at a table located on a picturesque patio beside a sharp curve in the road. Since we were too late for the plat du jour, we were offered a sandwich jambon. As I was taking a bite out of the sandwich, I noticed a line of traffic heading our way at what seemed to me to be an inordinate speed. At first I paid little attention to it, but as I chewed I realized a truck was heading straight toward our table. Sandwich in midair, frozen in half chew, I could feel the panic tightening my throat. Struggling to speak, I pointed in the direction of the oncoming vehicle. Lettie, Madeline, and Mona looked up from their sandwiches, horrified to discover the prospect of imminent obliteration. The oncoming truck bore down, swerving at the very last moment, in the curve of the road, passing less than five feet from where we were eating. We continued with our lunch, but it was a little unnerving. There you'd be, taking a bite out of your "sandwich jambon" as a milk truck or a Citroën sped toward you in midswallow. I hoped Lettie knew the French translation for Heimlich maneuver.

Dinner

Tagliatelli with Roasted Peppers in a Red Wine Tomato Sauce
Stuffed Eggplant
Poire Williams Sorbet
Gold–Dipped Chocolate Almonds
1996 Chinon

FOR DINNER I COOKED tagliatelli with a red sauce I made from a half pound of mushrooms, four cups of red wine, red and green roasted peppers, onions, garlic, two cups of water, a little olive oil, fresh basil and rosemary out of the garden, and two cans of tomato extract. The extract was thick like tomato paste, but had a taste and consistency that was denser. I had already browned the tomato extract in olive oil, added the rest of the ingredients, and was roasting the peppers over the gas jets when Lettie rushed into the kitchen.

"What's on fire? What's burning?" she asked, her voice rising in panic. Since it had been through her that the contact had been made, Lettie was, perhaps, the most anxious about the care of the house and its furnishings, but as the weeks went on, we all became increasingly protective, desiring to remain in the good graces of the owner and leave open the option to return.

"It's only dinner." I *tsked*.

When the peppers were finished, I baked miniature eggplants stuffed with their insides that I had scooped out and sautéed in olive oil with fresh basil, butter, and black pepper, mixed with the crumbs I made by grinding a leftover piece of baguette with hard Italian cheese. I baked them uncovered for about twenty minutes to a half hour at 400 degrees F. until they became a toasty brown on top.

For dessert we had Poire Williams sorbet, a sweet pear sorbet that was more like a pear gelato, and chocolate-covered almonds that had been dipped in gold. Naturally we had a bottle of lovely red wine, a 1996 Chinon.

After dinner, Helmut went out to the hall in back of the study to use the fax machine. He hadn't been gone long when we heard a sudden crash.

"What was that?" Lettie asked, a note of dread in her voice.

A moment later Helmut came into the kitchen rubbing his backside. "Um, *un petit problem*," he reported. "The chair just broke."

"Broke?" Lettie asked in alarm. "Which chair?"

"The one by the fax machine." Opening the refrigerator, he took the pink grapefruit juice from the shelf and poured himself a glass. "I was just sitting there and it broke!"

The rest of us rushed out to the hallway to inspect the chair.

"Do you think it's an antique?" Madeline asked. It looked like it was just an old chair painted white. But this was France; "old" might mean sixteenth or seventeenth century. Whatever the poor thing's age, it was certainly broken.

Helmut had carefully propped the back and its attached legs against the wall, with the rungs neatly piled beneath the seat on the floor.

"Maybe we should call the people that manage the house," someone suggested.

There was a moment of silence as we stood gathered over the broken remains of the unknown chair.

"Don't worry about me," Helmut called plaintively from the kitchen. "I'm all right. Nothing's broken."

"The chair is!" Lettie snapped back.

The rest of the evening was spent considering the different options for repairing the chair. Each of us suggested different scenarios: perhaps there was a place right here in town where it could be repaired, maybe we could find a shop in Tours. We continued fretting over this mishap for some time before finally dispersing back through the house without any resolution.

I turned on the television in hopes of hearing a weather report. However, the weatherman talked so fast none of us could understand him.

"They say that if cows are sitting down, that means it's going to rain," Helmut informed us with an air of authority. "I think when we get up tomorrow and look out the window, we should see if we can spot any cows. Then we'll know what the day will be like."

The rest of us stared at one another blankly, then quietly said good night and headed for our rooms. We could hear Helmut chortling.

———

Wednesday, July 22

Breakfast

Baguette French Toast with an Apricot Sauce

THE NIGHT BEFORE, I cut baguettes into three-inch chunks and
let them soak until morning in a mixture of four eggs, three
cups of milk, some vanilla, and a little nutmeg. By morning
all the liquid had been absorbed, so that each piece of bread
had to be lifted onto the buttered baking sheet with a slotted
spoon. I baked them in a preheated 400 degree F. oven until
they puffed up and became a golden brown. Melting down a
cup of apricot preserves with two ground fresh apricots, a little sugar, and a splash of Drambuie, I simmered the mix with

a few tablespoons of water until it became a sauce, then poured it over the buttered "French toast."

Over breakfast, Lettie returned to the question of the chair.

"Should we call Monsieur Dumont?" she asked.

"He's on vacation, remember?" Jack reminded her.

Helmut gritted his teeth in penitent apprehension.

~ ~ ~

LATER, AS I LOOKED out the upstairs window, I saw the herd of cows from the farm by the river.

"Hey, Helmut!" I called down into the garden where he was dragging an old canvas lawn chair from the storage cave. "Some of the cows are standing up, some are lying down. What do you think that means?"

"Possibility of scattered showers," he replied.

He set the chair up in the middle of the lawn and plopped himself down, immediately ripping through the canvas and ending up on the ground. Eyes wide, he looked up at me trying not to laugh, shaking his head from side to side. "Uh-oh, another petit problem," he said.

Lettie came out to the terrace to set the table for lunch, viewed the goings-on, and sitting down, defeatedly poured herself a glass of wine, muttering, "Ohhh, the hell with it."

Lunch

Tsatziki and Mixed Salad
1996 Vin d'Alsace Reisling

FOR THIS MEAL WE fixed sliced cucumbers mixed in yogurt and seasoned with salt, pepper, and garlic. There was a salad of lettuce, tomatoes, marinated green beans, and avocados in a dressing made with the juice of two lemons, about a quarter cup of corn oil, a good tablespoon of chopped garlic, a teaspoon or so of sugar, salt, and fresh crushed green peppercorns mixed into two cups of a rich sour cream. With it we ate a thick-crusted wheat bread and drank a bottle of 1996 Vin d'Alsace Reisling. The rest of the afternoon was spent in preparation for our first guests.

Simone and Abelard rang the gate bell punctually at four o'clock. We had set a table of fresh figs, apple slices, Camembert cheese from Normandy, the spicy-hot Moroccan olives, mousse de canard, a honey brandy called Hydromel, some goat cheese, an herbed cream cheese, and one leftover stuffed eggplant cut into bite-sized pieces.

Simone presented us with a basket of gifts: a loaf of packaged bread with a label that read *Méthode traditionelle, Domaine de Fleury*, a bottle of Bordeaux Chesnel, and a container of *la véritable Rillette du Mans* (shredded pork like we bought at the charcuterie the day we arrived), which she announced "was a specialty of the region."

Simone, a native of Tours, worked in administration in a hospital there. Abelard, an editor, was in advertising in Martinique, living part-time in Savonnieres, part-time on the island. It was his dream to ride a Harley-Davidson across Route 66 from Washington, DC, to California and down into Mexico. He spoke with such eagerness for this adventure that I wondered if his enthusiasm had begun with Marlon Brando's *The Wild One*, a cult hit in France in the fifties, and all those Hollywood movies that romanticized the image of the lonely rider, hair flying in the wind as he turns his "dust-laden metal steed into the eternal sunset of lonely but heroic adventure." I was about to suggest *Easy Rider*, but remembering everyone gets shot to death in the end, felt it might cast a pall on the pleasantries of the moment, to say nothing of Abelard's dream.

Expounding on the drama of negotiating precipitous cliffs, I urged Abelard to cycle Big Sur. "*La mer . . . ah, la mer*," I said, trying to convey the color of the Pacific. Unable to think of the French word for "*blue*" I resorted to Italian. "*Azure mare*," I said. Abelard looked puzzled then suddenly understood. "Ahh, *bleu*, like your eyes," he said with perfect aplomb. Hah, those French. It was one of the most charming compliments I had ever received. He had immediately endeared himself to me even if I felt a little stupid for not having known the French word for "blue" was *bleu*.

Our new friends were very winning. They spoke a little English, but with Lettie's and Mona's translations, we were able to keep the conversation flowing. We drank brandy and wine, ate the rillettes and cheese and figs, and passed a pleasant couple of hours in the bright light of the warm early evening. We were dissapointed to learn that they were leaving Friday for a two-week stay in Morocco and they wouldn't be back in time for us to see them again. As they left, Simone affectionately kissed each of us four times, twice on each cheek, "like Paris," she explained, and they bid us adieu.

Mona locked the gate after them and walked back up the drive to the terrace. "We've had company. We're here a week and we've already had company."

"I know," Madeline said. "I'm beginning to feel like we live here."

"Well, we are living here," Helmut added.

"It's like heaven," Jack chimed in with just a hint of saccharine.

There was a long pause.

"There are no exits in heaven," I said.

Dinner

Chicken Vegetable Soup with Homemade Noodles
Strawberries with Sugar and Crème Fraîche

LATER WE SAT DOWN to a light supper of soup made from last night's leftover chicken. After picking all of the meat from the carcasses, I boiled the bones to make a stock, discarded them, and added several thinly sliced carrots, a couple of cups of white wine, about a cup of celery chopped small, and four minced green onions. I seasoned the soup with salt and pepper, a little garlic, and some fresh thyme.

I broke an egg into a cup, added about two tablespoons of flour and mixed it to the consistency of molasses. Bringing the soup to a rolling boil, I took a large wooden spoon and began stirring until I had formed a circling eddy. Then I slowly dripped the egg-and-flour mixture into the edge of the boiling whirlpool, letting the motion cook the mixture into small dumplinglike noodles. My grandmother had taught me how to make these when I was five. She called them *kluskis*, Polish noodles.

For dessert we again ate strawberries with sugar and crème fraîche.

After dinner we sat on the terrace enjoying the evening color.

"Did you notice there are no screens for the windows?" Helmut asked.

"I did," I replied. "We noticed that the first day we were here."

"And nothing bites you," Madeline marveled.

"That's because there are no flies or mosquitoes in this area," Helmut continued sagely, "and those little moths that fly in at night fly right out as soon as you turn off the light."

How perfect!

Thursday, July 23

THIS MORNING, AFTER OUR usual feast of warm baguettes, croissants, and butter, Lettie, Jack, Mona, and I set out to find the château at Chenonceau. Helmut and Madeline had found two old bikes in the caves and, wanting to take a bike ride, declined to join our excursion.

It was wonderful to see the villages and towns en route, and we might have enjoyed a stop at any of them, but instead elected to press on and arrive at the château as early as possible. I was particularly sorrowful to have forgone a stop at the cloister where the renowned pastry pets-de-nonne is believed to have had its origin. Legend has it that a novice, preparing choux pastry, was caught off guard by an unexpected burst of flatulence and accidently dropped a piece of the dough into deep fat, thus producing a wonderfully light and airy delicacy. When naming the new pastry (a soufflé fritter filled with cream or jam), one of the nuns called it *pet-de-nonne* (nun's fart).

The ancient plane trees lining the allée along which you approach the château arched over us like the nave of a great cathedral. Entering the palace grounds, we decided it would be wise to eat now, just before the lunch hour began. The crowds were already gathering at what had once been the royal stables, since converted into public dining rooms. I held a table out in the busy courtyard while the others went inside to order.

The crowd at Chenonceau was the most international I had seen since arriving in France. There was a tour bus from Morocco that arrived soon after we did. A stream of interesting-looking people descended from the bus and sat down near us. Speaking at first what I thought was Arabic, they lapsed into another language that sounded like Hebrew and from there they jumped into French punctuated by an occasional English sentence. As people passed our table carrying trays of food, I recognized Japanese, Spanish, Italian, German, and of course, English—American and some British—being spoken as well. It was a great feeling to be a part of this mix.

Both Jack and I had chicken in a sweet-and-sour tomato sauce with peppers and onions, Lettie had a seafood dish and Mona, fearing she had been eating too much, lunched on a lovely tomato-and-avocado salad with a mayonnaise dressing.

From where we sat eating, I could look across the formal gardens first planted by Catherine de Medici to the wonderful gallery that spans the Cher, the same river on which our own village was located. Small *bateaux à rames* (rowboats) glided around huge stone pilings, which housed the château's three kitchens, conveniently serviced by their access to the water. The potted orange trees along the perimeter of the garden reminded me of the story I had heard about another de Medici, the famous Marie. While the four of us ate I related the tale.

It seems the queen was down with a terrible illness, a "malady" as they used to say, and the royal physicians called for the cooks and ordered them to simmer oranges with sugar as a remedy. The cooks began to refer to the mixture as "Marie's Malade," which eventually boiled down (no pun intended) to "marmalade."

From its earliest days, Chenonceau was noted for its sumptuous cuisine. Culinary legend tells us that when Marie de Medici came to live in France as the queen to Henri IV, she was so distressed by French cooking that she sent back to Italy for her own chefs to teach the French how to cook.

But Catherine arrived in France thirty years before Marie was even born and it was in her time that the castle gained its reputation for fine cooking. It was remarkable to think about this as I stood in the enormous double-leveled kitchens of the castle with their scores of copper pots, pans, molds, and tubs, the different sinks carved out of stone, the huge fireplaces, and the great wheel that brought in water from the river. If Chenonceau had a reputation for great food, Catherine must have had something to do with it, perhaps bringing her own chefs from Florence long before Marie arrived.

Of all the châteaux we visited, Chenonceau certainly had the most convenient, most workable and best-equipped kitchen, supporting my speculation that it was actually Catherine and not Marie, who could claim the legend.

Here possibly, I thought, is the very kitchen where those chefs cooked and the cuisine that we know as French really began.

We spent that afternoon happily touring this beautiful edifice. On our way out, we wedged our way through the crowds into the small gift shop at the bottom of the watchman's tower. Jack and I were in and out in about thirty seconds (I was hoping to find orange marmalade), but Mona and Lettie managed to spend a good half hour in search of that indefinable treasure all tourists seek in a foreign country. Mona, alas, came away with something else.

On the ride back to Savonnieres she began to feel somewhat uncomfortable. Reviewing what we had eaten that afternoon, Lettie remembered, "Wasn't there a mayonnaise dressing on your salad?"

"Oh God, please don't say that word," Mona pleaded, her hands held protectively over her stomach. "I know that's what made me sick."

By the time we reached the house, her stomach was reel-ing. Consulting the essential green book under the heading *Medical Emergencies,* we discovered that a doctor lived just next door, sharing a common wall with us. We had passed the house many times. Inside the gates a border of boxwood hedges enclosed a small, elegant courtyard with a gravel parking space and a perfectly manicured lawn.

Mona rang the bell at the gate and was invited into the front room that served as an office. The doctor listened atten-tively, gave her some pills, and wrote out a prescription for the local pharmacy, advising her to "eat small bowls of very ripe bananas, shredded peeled apples, cooked starchy vegeta-bles, rice, some pasta, and drink lots of water."

"How about oranges?" I asked. "Does he want me to boil down some oranges with sugar for you?"

Ignoring my query, Mona began telling us what a nice man the doctor was and marveling that he had charged only a hundred and twenty francs, about twenty dollars in Ameri-can money.

We were genuinely amazed and agreed, "What a wonder-ful place! A person can not only see a doctor when they need one, but can actually afford to be sick in this country!"

Dinner

Sausage and Red Wine Ragout
Baguettes
Chocolate with Hazelnuts

THIS EVENING, I PREPARED a lovely stew of blood and white sausages sautéed in olive oil and tomato paste. When the tomato paste was browned, I added potatoes, string beans, cauliflower, shallots, green onions, garlic, fresh thyme and chives, about a half cup of flour stirred well into the mix to form a kind of roux with the vegetables, about a cup of water (to unstick the pot), half a bottle of red wine, and some salt and pepper. I let it simmer, covered, until the potatoes were tender to the touch of a fork. We ate the stew with leftover baguettes from breakfast, sopping up the juices with the bread. For dessert we had chocolate bars with hazelnuts.

I say "we," but actually Mona had a "tasty" bowl of unseasoned rice with a little shredded apple and some water. France is not the place to be on a restricted diet. We steered her away from the hazelnut chocolate. She insisted, however, that the doctor told her she should drink a glass of red wine . . . or two.

Friday, July 24

BY THIS TIME THE morning routine was firmly established: set the table, put on the coffee, and head for the patisserie. Often I would get a variety of flavored croissants instead of plain ones, but the baguette was a must. It was an unceasingly perfect way to start the day.

Some days we just stayed at the house—painting, washing clothes, cooking, gardening, maybe going out for a short walk around town. There was never any great rush to get out onto the road to "see something."

Across the *rue* from us were five little houses all joined together, inhabited by people who looked almost as old as their houses. By this second week, these neighbors had begun to know us, although I'm certain from the moment we arrived they were aware of our every move.

The little dog who came out on to the windowsill to yell at us that first day now recognized and looked forward to seeing Lettie, who stopped to pet him every time she passed.

Monsieur Deek was his name.

One day, on the street, the little dog came up to Lettie, tail wagging, little snout pointed up, eyes half closed the way dogs do when they are blissed out, and rubbed against her leg. Lettie bent down and began scratching him under the chin.

"I am amazed," the old man who was his master commented. "He never takes to strangers like this. He must really like you." Suddenly the little dog turned around twice and lifted one leg in the direction of Lettie's shoe.

"*Oh! Monsieur Deek,*" the old man called. "*Non, non, non!*" Obediently the little dog put his leg down, chagrined, I'm certain, at being deprived of his affectionate gesture of claiming Lettie as his territory, and slowly, tail between his legs, headed back into the house, turning once to give the old man a dirty look over his shoulder.

The old man and his wife, a couple well into their eighties, had met during the Second World War in one of the local caves, where they had taken shelter from the bombardment. She was a refugee from the north of France and he was in the Greek army. Eventually they fell in love, and when the war was over they returned to Savonnieres, married, and moved into the little house across the street from us where they have since lived.

Every evening, Monsieur Deek would leave his house and walk a few doors up the street to visit with the aged lady who lived alone in the last house. He'd stay for an hour or so, chew on a little bone or dog biscuit, and then she'd open the door for him to return. The old man would be waiting at his open door and the two people would have a conversation as Monsieur Deek ambled the short distance, sniffing a step here, following a scent there.

Lettie and Mona, both dog owners, stopped in a hardware store one day to purchase one of the BEWARE OF THE DOG signs they had seen on so many fences and gates which, in French, actually says VICIOUS DOG ON GUARD. The salesperson told them they could no longer buy those signs. They had, in fact, been taken off the market because it had been deemed "unfair to make a negative judgment on the dog." It was the only incidence of "political correctness" I saw in France. Naturally, I was sympathetic.

Lunch

Mousse de Canard
Avocado, Ripe Tomatoes, and Onion Salad
Celeriac Rémoulade
Camembert and Chèvre
Baguettes
Petits Suisses with Ripe Peaches
Sparkling Vouvray

THERE ARE MOMENTS WHEN you feel that life has actually come together. Lunch this day was, for me, one of those moments. The weather was perfect, as it had been since we got there—clear blue sky, no humidity, temperature in the low eighties, bright sun, and a soft warm breeze. We set the table on the terrace with the blue-and-white Limoges. There were fresh baguettes, mousse de canard, ripe avocados, sliced red tomatoes, and onions. I had grated up a celeriac root and made a rémoulade by mixing it with a cup and a quarter mayonnaise, half a cup of Dijon mustard, two tablespoons of crushed garlic, the juice of a lemon, and a generous twist of fresh ground black pepper. There were two kinds of Camembert, some local goat cheese, and of course a great hunk of that wonderful butter. We drank a bottle of sparkling Vouvray, cold and just barely sweet, and for dessert we ate petits suisses with a little sugar and some juicy ripe peaches.

Sitting on the terrace, in the sunshine, beneath the boxwood umbrella, with music playing and all of us together so pleased and happy, eating wonderful food, drinking champagne, we became, as sometimes happens when people live together, an ideal companionship that in its harmony remains in the memory as a relic of simple happiness.

~ ~ ~

THAT AFTERNOON LETTIE, MONA, and Madeline walked into the village to mail some postcards. On a building set back from the street, toward the center of town, they noticed a sign advertising MIEL A VENDRE (honey for sale) and decided to stop. For twenty francs they got a quart-sized, plastic container of thick, cloudy honey.

Back at the house we gleefully removed the lid for our first taste. Given the abundance of lavender in the region, I had hoped the honey might carry its scent—the thought of lavender honey was almost euphoric to me.

"Does it smell like lavender?" I asked hopefully.

Mona inhaled deeply. Puzzled, she gave the container a second, suspicious sniff.

"Goats!" she said. "Does this smell like goats to you?"

We passed the container from nose to nose.

"I'll be darned."

"Hah—it does smell like a goat"

"Yep, that's goat, all right."

We began to consider different explanations for this mystery.

"Could the bees have come from a field where goats were grazing?" Helmut questioned. "Lying on the flowers that the bees gather the nectar from?" he continued lamely. "That might give the flowers a sort of goat flavor."

Our skepticism quickly rejected this possibility.

"Maybe the goats make honey in France?"

"Maybe the container had been used to store goat's milk and the smell never went away?"

"I don't know. I never smell the goat when I drink goat's milk."

"That's a point."

We never did discover why the honey, strong and delicious nonetheless, had the smell of goat. However, Mona's olfactory discovery had ruined the honey for me and I never ate it again. She'll tell you the reverse, that I was the one who said it smelled like goats and ruined the honey for her, but since she was still under the doctor's care, I cannot hold her accountable for remembering the truth.

Later on that same afternoon, Madeline and Helmut returned from a long bike ride and announced that they had found the train station on the other side of the river about a mile out of town. They had watched a train stop to discharge passengers but had seen no sign of a ticket office, and on the way back, stopped at the town hall to inquire where the tickets might be purchased.

Madeline approached the desk. *"Est-ce-qu'il ya un chemin à Tours?"* she inquired, thinking she had asked, "Is there a train to Tours?" but actually asking, "Is there a road to Tours?"

Puzzled, the official glanced out the window as if for confirmation, peered over his glasses, and answered a politely supercilious *"Mais oui, madame."*

At a nearby desk a clerk had stopped writing, his pen suspended in midair.

Madeline pressed on. *"S'il vous plaît, puis-j'acheter un billet pour le chemin?"* ("Please, can I buy a ticket for the road?")

Bewildered now, the official shook his head, and indicating the road outside the window, explained, *"Madame, il ne faut pas de billet pour utiliser les chemins."* ("Madame, you don't need a ticket to use the roads.") Puzzled now herself, but realizing she must have used the wrong French word for "train," Madeline began pulling an imaginary cord and offered a *"toot, toot."*

"Ahh, le train!*"* exclaimed the official, the word being the same in both tongues. The misunderstanding cleared up now, the clerk returned to what he was doing as the patient official explained to an abashed Madeline that she could either pay on board or, on the return buy a round trip ticket at the station in Tours.

Helmut, who had endured her reproaches about the chair fiasco, sat back with a look of contented vindication as she related this latest embarrassing miscommunication. We roared with laughter in appreciation of her dilemma. All of us had, at one time or another, suffered similar conversational confusions. One day while walking along a country road, I passed a farm where there grew an enormous hedge of lavender. It must have been five feet high. Thinking I was commenting on how beautiful it looked, I said to the woman working in the yard there, *"Votre lavage est jolie."* She nodded a gracious *merci*, but quickly retreated into the house.

"Lavande is the word for 'lavender,' " Mona told me as I

was recounting the story to her later. "*Lavage* means 'laundry' . . . you told the woman her wash was beautiful."

"Huh." I thought for a moment, surprised at the information. "There was no wash," I admitted.

"Well then," said Mona, matter-of-factly, "the woman probably thought you were nuts."

Dinner

Turkey Cutlets Baked in a White Wine and Emmenthal Cream
   Sauce
New Potatoes Fried with Cabbage
Green Beans Sautéed in Garlic and Olive Oil
Fresh Strawberries on Vanilla Ice Cream
Kir Royales

OUR FRIEND MANUEL HAD called to say he was due to arrive that afternoon from Paris and I wanted to make a lovely dinner in honor of his visit. I'd had the butcher slice seven paper-thin cutlets from a turkey breast, which I dipped in egg and milk, coated with a mixture of ground baguette crumbs and hard Italian cheese, and sautéed in butter and olive oil. After they were browned on both sides, I laid them in a baking dish and covered them with a sauce of three cups of whole milk mixed with Emmenthal cheese, shallots, salt and pepper, one cup of white wine, and with the leftover bread crumbs and egg wash added for a thickening, I put the dish into a 350 degree F. oven and baked them for twenty minutes.

Unfortunately, the sauce cooked too long and separated, but it was easy to remedy. Removing the cutlets onto a platter, I poured the liquid into the blender, whizzed it back into a cream sauce, and poured it over the turkey. I served thinly sliced new potatoes, fried with chopped cabbage in butter, salt and pepper, and fresh string beans, sautéed in olive oil and garlic.

Any green vegetable is made most desirable by simply sautéing it in some olive oil, butter and garlic, salt, and black pepper. You want to keep the fire a tad less than moderate, and you want to stir, or shake, the pan often. If the vegetable "scotches," as my grandmother used to say (now popularly referred to as caramelized), all the better, but be forewarned, it is a close call between caramelizing and burning.

For dessert we spooned fresh strawberries over a velvety vanilla ice cream and drank Kir Royales.

During dinner, Manuel told us that his trip to Paris had not turned out as planned. Although he had gotten the apartment, as promised, in exchange for some carpentry, the teacher he was going to study under had suddenly died, leaving him at loose ends but still committed to an agreement from which he felt he couldn't back out. We expressed our sympathies, but, Manuel conceded, it was not an awful fate to be stranded in Paris. We set him up in the study on the sofa bed and hoped the house would have the same effect on him as it was having on the rest of us.

Saturday, July 25

TOURS WAS CELEBRATING ITS annual garlic-and-basil festival that weekend in honor of the feast day of St. Anne, which was on Sunday, and after breakfast Helmut, on vacation from his shuttle service, shuttled the seven of us in two trips out to the station for an early train into the city.

A privet hedge ran along the back of the platform of the station, screening the garden of the little house that had been the stationmaster's (before automation). A black poodle began running frantically back and forth along its length, yapping at us until someone shouted at him from the house to shut up. The flowering shrubs of the garden made a pleasant backdrop to the three-sided passenger shelter for which we had little use on this fine morning. A breeze kept the mild air refreshing and clean, bending the grasses of the surrounding fields. On the other side of the crossing, a vacant farm was for sale. Its house and barn stood nearly flush to the road, the untended front yard romantically overgrown, with althea (a popular shrub in this area) planted on either side of the door. Across the tracks there was a small machine shop and more farmhouses a little bit beyond that.

Minutes before the train's arrival, a sign (attached to the shelter) lit up; a musical chord played, and a seductive and lovely-sounding woman began to speak in French. "*Bonjour, messieurs, 'dames,*" she said, and then, "step back from the tracks, please, the train will be arriving in exactly three minutes, stopping once before its final destination . . . *à Tours.*" The city's name was purred out in a particularly inviting manner: ". . . *à Toouurs.*" From this moment on, none of us was ever to speak the name again in our normal voices, preferring instead to mimic the elegant vowels of the lady on the recording, "*À Toouurrrs.*" I found myself comparing her with Amtrak conductors who garble out destinations over faulty microphones and loudspeakers that blare out not only what you can't understand, but fan your fear that you'll never make the right connection and end up in a horror movie.

The ten-minute train ride carried us though acres of truck farms surrounding great greenhouses in which grew different types of lettuce and other produce. Community gardens began to appear as we approached the city. The conductor walked through the short train announcing, *"Tours, bon voyage, Tours"* as the train slowed to a halt within the station.

We exited under the sweep of a vaulted glass ceiling. Pigeons soared through the girdered posts and rafters holding it aloft. Following along the platform, we entered a station decorated with ornate pilasters separating colorful wall tiles that depicted regional scenes—all accessible from that point of departure.

From there we strolled out into the square and along a pedestrian mall of stores to a shaded boulevard. We stopped for a drink at a café beneath one of the great plane trees lining the street before making our way toward le Vieux Tours, a section of fifteenth-century structures and Gallo-Roman excavations near les Halles, where the festival was being held. Crowds jammed the old ways in and around the market.

"My gosh," I exclaimed, "look at the garlic!"

I had never seen so much beautiful plump garlic. With papery white skin, stained with a bleeding purple color, it hung in braids, heaped in piles spread across the pavements, and even stacked artfully into high pyramids. Farmers hawked their wares, pushing wheelbarrows of garlic past Lilliputian forests of basil. The amount of basil and its vigorous condition were impressive: large-leafed; small-leafed; tiny-leafed basil that was purple and green; a mix of colors in pots and bushel baskets and planters and loose cut, stacked, or hanging from racks.

A procession made its way through the narrow streets, led by a magician. There were jugglers in medieval costumes, musicians blowing shrill clarions and beating on drums, followed by people costumed in rags, the women clutching babylike bundles to their hearts, their faces made up with the mark of the plague. At one corner, a man selling toys bonged passersby on the head with a long plastic mallet that squeaked when it hit, and in the little while that we watched, men and women, children and adults, young and old, all laughed good-naturedly at the indignity of his assault.

At one o'clock, we stopped at the café across from les Halles where we had eaten on our first visit into Tours. Still mindful of her recent malaise, Mona begrudgingly ordered tea with a little bun and some butter, Jack ate a sandwich jambon, and the rest of us had tomato, basil, and fresh mozzarella salads with a brioche.

During lunch, Mona and Madeline consulted a city map for the address of the Magasin de Chaussures—the shoe store recommended by the blue-shoed "gym" lady in Balin-Mire. Lettie had resolved to pick up the copper pots she had held in reserve at the *antiquités* shop, and hoping the little gray dishes I had admired would still be there, I invited myself to join her. After we settled up the check, we headed out, agreeing to meet at the station for the late afternoon train. We left Jack, Helmut, and Manuel sitting under the umbrella, enjoying another glass of wine, and that quintessential French pleasure—people watching from a sidewalk café.

The little gray dishes, I was delighted to find, had not been sold since we were last at the *antiquités*. I spent the rest of the afternoon with Lettie, lugging the copper pots and my dishes through numerous drapery, material, and linen stores from which she purchased nothing.

By six we were making our way back through the crowds, and reuniting with the rest of the party at the station, we boarded the six-thirty train for our short ride home to Savonnieres. Helmut, Manuel, Mona, and Madeline took the car, along with our goods, back to the house, but Lettie, Jack, and I chose to walk from the station.

We had never walked this stretch of road before, and as we rounded a bend it follows along the river, the town suddenly appeared, stretched out on the other side, looking postcard quaint with its Romanesque church and the line of pollarded trees along the embankment.

Jack and Lettie discussed the various plants and trees along the roadside. An occasional car would speed past, taking our attention from the view, as we stepped lively off the pavement. At the park along the river, a family sat drinking wine at one of the picnic tables on the beach above the dam, and waved as we walked past. The smell of the meat they were cooking on an open grill excited my hunger and I considered what to prepare for a late supper.

"This is so beautiful." Lettie sighed.

Our silence expressed a mutual accord.

Dinner

White Sausage Ragout with Red Wine, Basil, and Garlic
Chocolate
Espresso
1996 Vin de Pays de l'Agenais Cabernet Sauvignon

THERE WERE A FEW white sausages that I cut into one-inch pieces and then put into a pot that was heating with a little olive oil. As the sausages began to brown, I added about a half cup of tomato "extract" (paste) and stirred it over the heat so that the paste and the sausages browned together. Browning tomato paste always gives any sauce a depth of flavor.

When the sausage and tomato paste were a rich, dark brown color I added about four cups of a cheap red wine we had bought just for cooking, cut up some potatoes, string beans, and cauliflower, added about a cup of chopped shallots, two chopped, medium-size onions, two cups of water, and seasoned it, in honor of St. Anne, with copious amounts of garlic and fresh basil. I added salt and pepper, covered the pot, and turned the heat down between low and medium. I let it cook for about an hour, stirring now and again to keep it from sticking. When the potatoes were soft to the poke of a fork, I mixed a couple of tablespoons of flour into a cup of red wine until it was smooth and then carefully added it to the stew, stirring it all the time until the stock thickened up.

It was a perfect supper for the end of a busy day of walking and sightseeing. We drank a bottle of 1996 vin de pays de l'Agenais Cabernet Sauvignon, and for dessert we ate chocolate and drank espresso.

After supper we read aloud from *The Country of the Pointed Firs*, a collection of vignettes about life in a nineteenth-century coastal Maine village. Its author was Sarah Orne Jewett, who was born, lived, and died in South Berwick, and one of the book's earliest translations had been undertaken by the French. It was intriguing to consider these very American tales from the perspective of this foreign country, which had been among the first to appreciate them. As I sat listening, I found my attention wandering, imagining the French counterparts, in a rural village like Savonnieres, of the sea captains, merchants, and farmers of Jewett's "Dunnett's Landing."

Sunday, July 26

SELECTING THIS TIME OF year for our stay—July 15 to August 15—couldn't have been a better choice. The weather was perfect. Marie-Claire told us that before we arrived it had rained almost every day for a couple of weeks. Once, on our second or third day, there was a slight shower a little before noon—so brief, like a mist, the sun didn't even disappear. Occasionally I thought I could hear rain in the middle of the night, but by morning the sun was bright and the sky cloudless.

The temperate climate and abundance of exotic plants made us feel as though we had gone south, when, in fact, we had traveled farther north. It occurred to us that since the summer light was so long at this latitude—dawn was at five, darkness didn't arrive until ten at night—the winter might effect the reverse. Calculating the seasonal differences, I thought the sun would not rise until ten in the morning and might set at three-thirty in the afternoon.

Heaven may have no exits, but it could have a darker side.

~ ~ ~

OVER THE LONG SUNNY days, the pattern of eating constantly changed, with the exception of breakfast, which was always around seven or eight, lingering sometimes until eleven or eleven-thirty. Since we were not obligated to anything, we might eat a lunch at noon or one o'clock, and have a meal at six or seven. Sometimes we would eat a late lunch at three or four in the afternoon and then at ten have a full sit-down dinner. It changed from one day to the next.

An Early Dinner

Roasted Herb Chicken
Pasta in a White Wine and Bell Pepper Sauce
Curried Peach–and–Pear Orange Custard Tart

I CUT THREE CHICKENS down the center into halves, rubbed them all over with a mixture of olive oil, herbes de Provence, garlic, salt, and a generous amount of fresh-ground black pepper. Laying them in the earthenware baking dish, I slipped them into a preheated 450 degree F. oven and let them brown for about fifteen to twenty minutes.

While the chickens were browning, I minced up four whole ripe tomatoes with a red bell pepper, a yellow bell pepper, and a large onion and spread it over the browned chicken with a half bottle of white wine, covered the dish and put it back in the oven, turning the heat down to 375 degrees F. to cook for almost an hour. After the chickens had cooked, I lifted them onto a platter, boiled up enough bow-tie pasta for all of us, and tossed it into the leftover chicken sauce with some fresh basil and Parmesan.

For dessert I made a curried-pear-and-peach tart. The dough was a butter pastry made with a half pound of butter, two-and-some cups of flour, three tablespoons of ice-cold Perrier, one egg, and a handful of sugar. I did it all in the food processor, and once again I didn't roll it out but pushed it around in the tart dish by hand. I peeled and sliced the peaches and pears and laid alternating slices around the dough until it was filled. I think I used about three of each fruit.

Then I made a mixture of a cup of sugar, two tablespoons of curry, a half cup of orange juice, six eggs, and a quarter cup of melted butter and spread it over the fruit. I baked it for almost an hour at 325 degrees F. What emerged from the oven was a tart filled with sweetened fruit sitting in a lightly curried orange custard. When we cut into the tart, it was still warm, and we finished it in one sitting.

After dinner, Jack and I went out for a bicycle ride. We

rode through town to the bridge where the Marina Café was, crossed over, and headed south following the river. The houses along the road were beautiful. All of them were of stone, most built a few hundred years before, but even the ones that were relatively new, built in this century or perhaps even this decade, harmonized with their surroundings. Nothing looked out of place.

An old woman in a large straw hat tied with a scarf was cutting lavender and roses in her walled garden and putting them into a basket on her arm. She reminded me of one of the drawings in a Mother Goose book I had as a child and I called out, *"Bonjour, madame,"* as we rode by. She smiled and returned, *"Bonjour, monsieur."*

To be away from everything you know, including language, telephones, a work schedule, television, newspapers, and your everyday routine was more liberating than I could possibly have imagined. The freedom made me feel younger, not in the sense of youthfulness, but in the sense of being more expectant of a future that held promise. I think that feeling happens to anyone who can completely throw himself out of the familiar and into the unknown. You simply need to put the plan into action. It's like cooking. Once you heat up the pan, all you have to do is put something in it and it becomes a meal. The more you add, the more you care, the sooner a meal becomes a banquet. I thought about this as we rode farther into the countryside.

≈ ≈ ≈

I WAS BORN INTO families of great-aunts and grandmothers who were incredible cooks. Plain and simple, salt-and-pepper cooking both on the Polish and the Scotch-English-German side. These women always made me feel welcome in the kitchens—to "lick a dish," cut an onion, drop cookie dough onto the cookie sheet, or stir the pots. I learned to make noodles at five years old, but didn't eat a soufflé until I was twenty-three. I was taught how to make milk soup at six, but didn't eat a lobster until I was twenty-five. By sixth grade I was buying boxed cake mixes and adding all kinds of things to them just to see what would happen: grape Kool-Aid in an angel-food mix, or strawberry jam instead of sugar in a chocolate cake and orange juice in brownies. Even at that age, I simply loved and understood food and cooking.

From the first day I walked into my kitchen at the restaurant, I possessed an innate comprehension of ingredients, quantities, heat, and how to add different things to the everyday edibles to create something new. Perhaps it had to do with growing up in a working-class family during the war years of the forties, watching my mother "stretch" the soup, turning a handful of leftover potatoes into potato pancakes, never throwing anything away but using it up until it became a stew or Spanish rice, or a casserole, making a whole new taste each time a leftover was used. It is a vanishing art. Most of all I understand taste. That's really the bottom line. If it's food and it doesn't taste good, what have you got?

Food, not music, is the universal language to me. You don't need to understand a person's language to know what he is doing when you watch him cook. One evening I watched two chefs on French television making a pâté de fois gras, and while I couldn't understand a word of their explanations, I completely understood everything they were doing. I felt akin to their culture of food and cooking. Not like an outsider, someone who was not a part of the schooled elite, but a fellow *cuisinier*.

Having never become the serious playwright or novelist that had been my youthful ambition, I had come to think of cookbooks as a lesser form of writing. But here, in this land of beautiful food and wonderful cooking, quite unexpectedly it occurred to me that all I *wanted* to write about was food. It was, as the French would say, my *métier*.

Dinner

Chicken Pasta Salad
Camembert with Baguettes
Chocolate Hazelnut Bars

BY EIGHT-THIRTY WE had begun to feel hungry again, so I made a salad out of the leftover chicken. I picked the meat from the bones, mixed it in with the pasta that was left over,

added a chopped onion, a little celery, and some fresh tomatoes and peppers, olive oil, enough lemon juice to make it
"salady," more garlic, and some salt and pepper. We served it
with leftover baguettes from the morning, two kinds of
Camembert, and a bottle of wine. It was perfect for that time
of night.

For dessert we ate chocolate hazelnut bars.

After dinner, Mona suggested, or, more accurately,
harangued us, into playing a game of Pictionary. None of us
was that interested, but since she was still convalescing from
her illness, we acquiesced out of sympathy. Without getting
too much into the particulars, I noticed with interest how the
darker side of personalities can arise during friendly competi-
tion, even when one of those personalities is recuperating. As
for myself, I am not competitive . . . as long as I'm winning.

Monday, July 27

Breakfast

Spanish Omelet with Potatoes and Shallots

I RETURNED FROM THE patisserie to find Lettie parboiling potatoes for a Spanish omelet. When the potatoes were partly cooked, she drained them and sautéed them in olive oil with shallots until they were soft. She whipped up a dozen eggs with about a quarter cup of cold water and poured them over the potatoes. Adding a cup of grated Gruyère over the top, she covered the pan and turned it on low until it had solidified and the cheese had melted.

Over breakfast, Manuel confessed that he had fallen in love with the house in his short stay here and was reluctant to return to Paris that afternoon. From the beginning, he had opted out of our plan to find this rural retreat, preferring the opportunities and the "excitement" of the big city. The rest of the morning was spent simply enjoying the garden, and by one-fifteen we bid Manuel a fond farewell and Helmut drove him to the train.

We decided it might be a nice change to eat lunch at the slightly more upscale restaurant and inn at the corner. The green book was not overly enthusiastic about it, but did say it was under new ownership and hesitated to make a pronouncement about the food. It was the attractive, ivy-covered building sitting right at the entrance to the town. It was into its parking lot that the police had pulled us the day we had arrived.

We were ushered into the garden by a somewhat stern and unsmiling hostess and seated under a canopy at a long table covered in a red cloth. The waitress arrived and we ordered small carafes of red and white wine. Our selection was complicated by her insistence on practicing her execrable English on us, even though Lettie's French was much better.

The menu offered regional dishes. Helmut and Lettie both had a fois gras as an appetizer and duck breast for their main course, along with zucchini in a savory nutmeg custard. I started with a terrine of salmon, then pintadeau forestier (guinea fowl in a rich brown sauce), while Madeline and Mona also had the salmon with a crûdité for a first course.

Jack ordered boeuf à la maison with green vegetables. For dessert we ate pear tarts and crème caramel.

The lunch turned out to be just okay. The price, almost twenty dollars apiece, took us all over our frugal budgets, but we agreed it was nice to be eating out for a change, though everyone said they liked my cooking better. (Even in a foreign country, smart people know which side of their *pain* their *beurre* is on.)

≈ ≈ ≈

LATER THAT AFTERNOON I took my usual long walk, crossing the main road to the lane that led out into the fields. On my left, and just as you entered the town, was a camping area on the riverbank. A man was shaving, using a mirror hung from a low branch of a tree, a pan of water sitting on a stump next to him. Beyond him a woman was wringing out clothes and spreading them over bushes to dry while her husband leaned against the car and read, keeping one eye on a crawling baby. Some boys were kicking a soccer ball while their parents sat patiently with a fishing pole on the banks of the river. On the other side of the road, on the tennis courts, a young couple vigorously batted a ball back and forth, while nearby a group of elderly men played a boccilike game called *pétanque*. Wielding crochet hooks and knitting needles to the tempo of their rapid conversation, their wives sat on benches in the shade, keeping one eye on the pattern, the other on the game.

Paralleling the river, the road continued for a quarter of a mile, entering into the fairgrounds where a grid of poplars had been planted in perfect alignment. Walking beneath them, I felt I had entered into a great hall held aloft by a hundred pillars of standing timber. The fields of sunflowers and corn that surrounded the fairgrounds were irrigated by compressors that pulled up water from the river through long pipes to numerous sprinklers, and everything, despite the dry weather, was green and healthy. The fields had recently been cut, the hay rolled into giant bales that sat in the fields like those enormous heads on Easter Island.

The road turned to gravel and I continued to follow it, skirting open fields, passing through shaded groves, following the river farther north until I could hear machinery from the mill—Moulin Balin—in the distance. Dotting the road at irregular intervals were weekend houses with fenced-in gardens—usually small, one-room affairs, often little more than a shack, where people would come from the city and spend a weekend tending their vegetables, sleeping in the sheds or under the stars in sleeping bags, and cooking on a grill in the open. Occasionally the sheds were a little more upscale, with perhaps two rooms instead of one. I recall seeing the name *petit moulin* ("little mill") painted artfully on the wall of one such place.

The three-storied, gray-colored, limestone Moulin Balin sat at a bend of the river. The huge, faded red waterwheel that for three hundred years had turned the grinding stone was still. A modern, more efficient building had been added across the road from it, and I could see men packing bags with that milled flour that makes the baguette taste so different from anything baked at home. At the base of the original mill, a few men sat quietly and fished. In the many peaceful scenes I witnessed in the month I was in France, I don't ever remember the intrusion of a boom box disturbing the serenity. There seemed to be a universal appreciation of quiet. Not a single car passed me on the road back, and except for a hiker carrying a full pack, a little dog wagging its tail in greeting, and a farmer who waved from his baler, I walked in perfect solitude.

~ ~ ~

MADELINE, HELMUT, AND JACK were in the kitchen when I returned. They told me Mona and Lettie had gone down to the river to paint.

"We want to find out if we can get married while we're here," Madeline announced. She and Helmut had been discussing it with Jack when I arrived.

"We were just on our way down to the church to talk with the priest."

"I'm astonished," I replied.

"So am I," Helmut concurred.

This was already toward the end of their time here. It was Wednesday and they would be leaving on Sunday. When the priest with whom they spoke told them it was impossible to marry on such short notice, he suggested, instead, an engagement blessing, which he would be most happy to perform. They agreed and the date was set for Friday, the twenty-ninth, at six-thirty in the evening.

Dinner

Meat Loaf Cheval
Oven–Browned Potatoes
Green Beans Sautéed in Olive Oil and Garlic
Crème Caramel
Cabernet Sauvignon

WHEN I SUGGESTED MEAT loaf, everyone applauded. The meat, ground fresh for me when I ordered it, was better looking than any ground beef I had ever bought—a deep rich red with very little fat content. I minced up a red pepper, an onion, and some garlic, made about a cup of bread crumbs from a piece of leftover baguette ground with rosemary from the garden, and added it all to the meat with a couple tablespoons of olive oil, half a cup of melted butter, two eggs, and salt and pepper. Forming it into a loaf, I placed it in the earthenware baking dish and slipped it uncovered into a 475 degree F. oven for twenty minutes, then reduced the heat to 350 degrees F. to cook slowly for another hour.

Lettie offered to make oven-browned potatoes. She peeled enough potatoes for the six of us, then cut them into quarters like fat french fries and parboiled them. After a few minutes she drained them and tossed them into equal amounts of olive oil and butter, about a half cup of each, salt and pepper, and a little thyme from the garden, then placed them in the oven in a baking dish next to the meat loaf, turning them from time to time to brown them on all sides. Again we ate string beans.

Meat loaf, oven-browned potatoes, and string beans. It sounds so American, and yet it tasted deliciously different from what we were used to. Possibly because the ground beef, I later realized, had actually been ground horse. Only now do I dare reveal the truth. We drank a bottle of Cabernet Sauvignon and for dessert we ate crème caramel, providing Mona with six more of the little jars she had taken to saving.

WE WERE OFF UNUSUALLY early this morning. Madeline and Helmut were taking the car for an overnight stay on the Atlantic coast a couple of hours away and, before leaving, shuttled the rest of us to the station to catch the early train to Tours.

We arrived in the city before anything had opened and stopped for a little breakfast at the Café de l'Univers in the Hôtel Univers, where we enjoyed warm brioche with butter, jam, and coffee, looking out across the square to the opulent city hall on one side and the courthouse on the other. Working people hurried along the streets while double-sized buses with an accordion-pleated center that allowed them to maneuver the corners more efficiently deposited and picked up passengers. A young man riding what appeared to be a motor-scooter-vacuum-sweeper sped around the perimeter of the square, cleaning litter from the sidewalks and gutters.

On the way to the *toilettes* I passed through a darkened dining room and, looking up, was stunned to discover a magnificent vaulted ceiling of stained and painted glass depicting a mythological hunting scene. Before leaving, I brought the others back to see this superb work of art. As we stood there in the dimness, marveling at the representation, the waiter suddenly turned on all the lights, including the chandeliers, proudly illuminating the space as though a grand ball were about to be held. The date in a corner read 1898.

≈ ≈ ≈

THE TWO SISTERS LOOKED forward to a day of shopping. Having already done time waiting outside numerous gift shops for them (joining, temporarily, those legions of glassy-eyed husbands holding bags like souls lost in ennui), we feigned interest, but begged off in favor of a Delacroix exhibition that was being advertised all over Tours.

"Maybe we'll see you there later," Mona offered.

"Great," I replied, knowing full well they'd never make it.

"The train is at one-thirty," Lettie reminded us, "so if we don't catch up with you at the museum, don't forget to meet us at the station." We gave the usual warnings about traffic, getting lost, and spending too much money, and headed for the Musée des Beaux-Arts.

Located beside the Cathedral of Tours, the museum had

been constructed during the seventeenth and eighteenth centuries as the bishop's palace. In the courtyard was a great cedar of Lebanon, its sweeping lower branches, themselves thick as trunks, were supported by crutchlike braces. We had seen these magnificent trees before grouped as a backdrop to the rose-and-lavender parterre at Chenonceau, but this was by far the most impressive specimen. Planted in 1802, the girth of its trunk would have required four people, arms outstretched, to encircle the base.

Delacroix's brother had lived in Tours and the exhibition was of landscapes taken from the pages of a sketchbook the artist had kept during one of his many visits to the region. We were curious to see if any might be recognizable from the localities of our own frequent walks. The drawings, some of them scribbled over with notations about color and composition, were wonderful to see, but, I confess, it was really another work that I remember most.

Located in one of the upper rooms of the palace, it occupied two-thirds of a great space of wall and depicted a boy, perhaps eight or ten years old, in a desert waste, his arms encircling a young woman, her head buried in her hands in a gesture of despair. The title engraved on the plaque was *Hagar and Ishmail*. I was deeply moved by the young mother and her child in their cruel and desolate exile and I stood staring at the painting for a long time, trying to understand why I felt such empathy. Maybe all men, at one time or another, have been little boys futilely trying to protect their mothers from the desert of sorrow. Maybe it was just me try-ing to protect my own mother from the exile of life's ending.

On the way back to the station we ran into Lettie and Mona scrutinizing old boxes in a shop on the Rue des Antiquités. Mona happily opened her bags to show us her prized purchases—some exotic-looking lingerie and a pair of thick-soled, wedgie-like shoes with multicolored spaghetti straps across the toe and instep.

Her husband, Mackie, and their son, Rory, were arriving in a few days, and I said, "If you're planning on making Mackie crazy when he gets here, that outfit ought to do it."

It certainly worked for the shop owner, who, overhearing the conversation and eyeing the lingerie, grinned from ear to ear and exclaimed, *"Oo-la-la!"*

"See that," Mona reproached, "now here's another place in France I can never go back to again."

≈ ≈ ≈

WE ARRIVED BACK IN Savonnieres in time for the plat du jour at the Marina Café. Whenever we stopped there for a little lunch, the food was exceptional. The Marina was becoming a favorite place. Again the lunch was first class, and the cook, when she had brought our food, seemed pleased (and perhaps a little surprised) that I had recognized the mix of vegetables as ratatouille. I found myself comparing the food here with the more expensive inn down the road where we had eaten yesterday. When you eat at a small, inexpensive café and the food is okay, it's acceptable. If, on the other hand, you go out and spend a little more for a meal and it's just okay, it's a disappointment. However, when the food in the small café turns out to be more than you expected, you really have a prize. Such was the case with the Marina Café.

When Madame la Cuisinière brought dessert, she also brought her grandson to meet us. He was probably about three years old, with thick hair the color of licorice and eyes so dark and seductive you could not help but melt. Following his grandmama's directions, he held out his hand to each of us in turn and, bowing slightly, said, *"Bonjour, monsieur, bonjour, madame,"* executing each gesture in a most gentlemanly manner. His grandmama, like grandmothers everywhere, beamed with pride at the effect of her tutelage. We were entirely captivated.

The rest of the afternoon was spent quietly. Jack was reading, Lettie and Mona had gone off to the river to paint again, and I walked down to the little market in town. I have to admit I like food shopping almost as much as I like food cooking.

Dinner

Turkey Cutlets Stuffed with a Mushroom Pilaf in a White Wine and Sorrel Cream Sauce
Fresh Tomatoes in a Basil Dressing
Chocolate–Mango Ice Cream

TURKEY CUTLETS WERE BOTH delicious and the least expensive cut of meat (foul, actually) and always within the budget. Fortunately none of us ever tired of them. The trick is to make the turkey taste different each time you cook it. This evening I stuffed the cutlets with a mushroom pilaf, and baked them in a fresh sorrel and white wine cream sauce.

First I heated up the frying pan with a few tablespoons of olive oil, adding a couple cups of uncooked rice to it to brown. It's important to move the rice around either with a spoon or by shaking the pan while it's frying so that it doesn't burn. While the rice was browning, I set three cups of water to boil with a half a cup of butter, and chopped up about a cup each of fennel, onions, and red pepper. When the water was boiling I poured it over the rice. It really sizzles up when you do this, so you have to add it gradually. Then I added the chopped vegetables along with two cups of mushrooms. I seasoned it all with salt, pepper, garlic, and fresh rosemary, turned the heat down, and let it simmer until the rice had cooked. I laid out the cutlets and divided the rice mixture evenly among them, then rolled them up and put them into the clay baking dish. I poured a couple of cups of dry white wine in the dish, making certain the cutlets were covered, then sealed up the dish with aluminum foil and put it into a 400 degree F. oven. After about forty-five minutes, I removed the cutlets, drained the juices into a saucepan, added two cups of light cream and a bunch of chopped sorrel, salt and pepper, a little flour for thickening, and simmered the sauce until it was rich and creamy. I then poured the sauce over the cutlets and served them alongside a salad of fresh tomatoes with a basil dressing.

To our surprise, Madeline and Helmut appeared just as we were sitting down to eat. Helmut was ecstatic not to have missed dinner.

The coast was admittedly beautiful, but "it's nicer here," Madeline reported, explaining the decision to alter their original plan to stay overnight. They had brought me a bag of deliciously scented fennel salt from the salt flats of the Brittany coast and told us about the city of Saumur, which they had visited on their way home.

"It's just an incredibly beautiful place," Madeline enthused. "Like a tiny hunk of Paris had been plunked down in the middle of nowhere." Finishing the last of the dessert, chocolate-mango ice cream from the patisserie in Balin-Mire, Helmut agreed.

"And you know what else?" Madeline continued, directing her comments in particular to Mona and Lettie. "Lace!" The sisters froze to attention, a flaring of the nostrils being just perceptible. "We saw lace shops all over the place."

"How far is it?" Mona asked.

"About a two-hour ride from here," Madeline answered.

"An hour and thirty minutes," Helmut corrected.

"Is there a train?" Lettie asked.

"Not from Savonnieres," Helmut explained. "You have to go into Tours, *but* . . . I figured it all out." The professional chauffeur had emerged once again. "There's a train that stops in Langeais, just south of here. We could drive to Langeais then take the train from there."

"Should we go, then?" Jack asked.

Everyone thought that we should, and with Mack and Rory arriving in two days, and Helmut and Madeline's engagement ceremony and dinner scheduled for Friday, and their departure coming Sunday, we all agreed, "Tomorrow, then."

THAT MORNING THE PATISSERIE was offering a huge, lumpy-looking bread with a thick dark crust. The lady wrapped it in white paper for me and I carried it home in hungry expectation. It was absolutely delicious, but I was thankful I had a brilliant dentist. It was a tough, thick-crusted peasant wheat bread called *pain de soleil* ("bread of the sun") that we ate with plum jam, butter, and lots of black coffee.

After this scrumptious breakfast, the six of us piled into the car for the ride to Langeais: Helmut and Lettie in the front, the four of us jockeying into our regular positions in the back: Jack on one side with Mona squinched between his legs on the edge of the seat, me jammed into the other side, and Madeline riding sidesaddle on the hump in the center, my knee pressed into her back.

"Everybody comfortable?" Helmut asked.

We set off, driving southwest out of the village into a countryside of peach and apple orchards. At the tiny village of Lignier, a policeman stood at a crossroads directing traffic around a not-so-serious accident.

"Squinch down, Madeline," I directed, worried that he might pull us over for being overcrowded.

"If I squinch down any further I'll be dragging my culottes on the road," she replied.

"Let's all look the other way," I suggested, "and maybe he won't notice us."

Just as we were about to pass, the policeman turned in the opposite direction and Helmut gunned past and around the corner, chauffeuring us safely away from a potentially annoying confrontation.

The fifteenth-century castle of Langeais loomed high above the city like a dark sentinel, creating the strong sense of a place suspended in time, as though nothing had changed in five hundred years. In the town beneath, the narrow, busy streets were already filled with tourists.

The train station might have been a remnant from the earliest days of rail travel. It seemed everything had remained unchanged, the wooden benches in the waiting room, the wrought iron covering the stationmaster's cage, and the trim of stained and leaded glass of the windows were all intact. The stationmaster himself looked as though he had been imported from another era.

We took our places behind a young man engaged in lengthy negotiations, complicated by the difficulties the agent was having with the single, glaring concession made to these latter days of the twentieth century: an enormous computerized ticket machine. Following an intense exchange, the agent scrupulously pecked the young man's request into the contrivance. For some minutes nothing appeared. Perhaps giving a suggestion, the young man said something more and the agent pressed another key, and waiting, stared quizzically into the enormous screen for a response.

Lettie impatiently checked her watch with the time on the station clock.

Finally the tickets were printed out. The young man paid and sat down adjusting earphones to his head for his CD player, and within moments began tapping out an erratic rhythm on the venerable bench.

Continuing to stare into the blank screen as if trying to determine what had just occurred, the agent finally shook his head and greeted Lettie. *"Bonjour, madame."*

We were beginning to feel concerned that we might miss the train.

Lettie asked for six round-trip tickets, second class, on the next train to Saumur.

The agent methodically repeated the same slow process—typing her request into the machine, waiting patiently in silence for it to reply. At last the six tickets were printed out.

With less than five minutes before the train was to arrive,

Helmut suddenly decided *this* would be a good time to buy tickets for their return trip to Paris on Sunday.

"Helmut," Madeline pleaded, "we'll never get out of here."

Ignoring her entreaties, Helmut told the man what he wanted. Again the agent began the lengthy procedure. We could hear the sound of an approaching train in the distance. Fearing we would miss it, and casting loyalty aside, the rest of us hurriedly crossed over the tracks, where we waited, anxious that Helmut and Madeline might not join us in time. With moments to spare, the two of them emerged from the lobby as, simultaneously, the stationmaster stepped out from his office by a side door. I could hear the train speeding toward us. Madeline and Helmut waved, and were about to cross to our side when the ticket agent stepped before them with outstretched arms, blocking their way.

"*Restez ici,*" he told them calmly as the express train roared past at an incredible speed on the track they were just about to cross. In a state of shock, Madeline and Helmut realized they had narrowly missed becoming pâté. The ticket agent strolled away, calling back a serene "*bon voyage*" as they crossed to us. Moments later the train to Saumur arrived and we were safely on our way.

≈ ≈ ≈

ON THE OUTSKIRTS OF Langeais, Helmut pointed out a line of troglodyte dwellings he had seen with Madeline the day before, in the cliff face of the hillside overlooking the river. The mouths of the caves had been carefully fitted with stuccoed walls through which opened brightly painted doors and shuttered windows with gaudy flower boxes. There are many of these intriguing houses throughout the region, remaining after a thousand years, as human habitations, now with TV antennas bolted into the rock face and Fiats, instead of primordial beasts, harnessed outside.

The train sped us on through the broad valley of the Loire, crossing from Touraine into the region of Anjou. Long before we had arrived in the city, the great château de Saumur appeared as a distant eminence, seeming to overlook the great world in its entirety. There were few places in the beautiful vista, which had opened before us, that were undominated by this imposing landmark.

The train station was located on the other side of the river. Once again it was a glorious day, with a soft, temperate breeze and high cloudless sky, and we determined to hike across the long bridge that spans the Loire into Saumur.

The city was as Madeline had described it. From the bridge it appeared unified and compact, clearly bounded by the agrarian landscape through which the train had carried us. The beauty of its stone and the skill with which it had been worked to build the embankment, pavings, houses, and churches presided over by the great château, created that extreme refinement of urban space that makes French cities so distinctive.

By this time I was hungry again, and all for stopping at the first bistro we passed after the bridge. But Madeline and Helmut urged us on, directing us through the wonderful streets to a square dominated by the twelfth-century church of St. Pierre and surrounded by a cluster of outdoor cafés. By this time I was starving and began salivating over a café sign offering the PLAT DU JOUR: LAPIN.

Hot dog! I thought. Rabbit for lunch. A couple of waiters stood outside gossiping under the shade of an awning.

"*Six personnes, s'il vous plait,*" I said.

One of the waiters lifted his arm and pointed to the watch on his wrist. "*Fermé!*"

It was five past two by the clock in the steeple, but at a second café we could see there were people still ordering. The waiter waved us over, seated us, and announced the available choices: sandwich jambon, croque-monsieur, or croque-madame. By this time we were just about "sandwich-jamboned" out, so we all ordered the croques. Whatever they might be, we thought, at least it wouldn't be another ham sandwich. The waiter brought a couple carafes of red wine and we all settled down for a leisurely lunch. To our great amusement, when the croques appeared, the "monsieur" turned out to be a ham sandwich, open-faced, but with toasted cheese; the "madame" was the same *but* garnished with a fried egg.

After lunch, Jack and I took the long walk up the hill to the château. The view from the castle was magnificent, with a complete command of the surrounding landscape and the Loire, stretching for miles, north and south.

In the courtyard, we stopped to rest and watched a young boy, perhaps three or four years old, having what must have been the worst day of his young life. Whatever it was his parents and big sister wanted, he didn't. What had precipitated his fury must have occurred before our arrival. He was, by this point, beyond speech, wailing and stomping the cobbled paving. Maintaining a calm distance, his parents and the girl continued examining the different points of interest around the courtyard, never far off, never out of his sight. Now and again his mother would attempt to coax him back into joining them. This only infuriated him more. From the entrance leading down into the dungeons she called what might have seemed the final invitation at a point of departure. His tantrum suddenly exhausted, he relented, quieted himself, and begrudgingly trotted over to join them. Later, as we were making our way through the castle, we kept crossing paths; the little boy, being carried by his father now, was subdued but sullen still.

What impressed me most about this scene was that no one, not in the courtyard, or on the balconies, or in the tower, seemed to mind. It was as though everyone understood what being three is and were willing to make the necessary allowances.

At five o'clock we met back at the square as planned, with time enough for a last cool drink before the six-thirty train back to Langeais. There we compared our purchases of the day. I had bought two little handblown cordial glasses I'd seen in the window of a shop we'd passed on our way back from the castle, and Madeline had found a sleeveless blouse nicely trimmed in lace. Lettie and Mona had purchased antique kitchen curtains, but much to everyone's surprise, no lace!

Exhausted from all the walking, the sisters splurged on a cab back across the river while the rest of us made a fast hike to the station. As wonderful as it is that all the trains are on time, if you're late you've missed it. Luckily we arrived with time to spare. Back at Langeais, we again stuffed ourselves into the little car and headed home to Savonnieres.

Dinner

Turkey Ragout in a White Wine Cream Sauce
Baby Leek and Avocado Salad
Pain de Soleil
Chocolate and Crème Caramel
Vin Rouge

I CUT THE LEFTOVER turkey from last night's dinner into small pieces, put the pieces into a pot to cook with chopped red and green bell pepper, two medium-sized sliced onions, the left-over sorrel cream sauce, another two cups of white wine mixed with a couple of tablespoons of flour, three or four carrots sliced thin to cook quickly, and a great handful of green beans, and simmered it into a creamy stew.

Lettie put together a salad of lettuce, ripe tomatoes, baby leeks from the garden, and an avocado, with a dressing made of wine vinegar and a mix of olive and corn oil. We ate the last of the pain de soleil, drank a bottle of red wine, and relaxed after dinner with chocolate bars and crème caramel.

Mackie and Rory would be arriving tomorrow. This was to be the first time we would all be together since our last dinner in the States. We were all excited about this reunion and Mona was anxious to have a lovely dinner waiting for them.

"Maybe we should have a roast of some kind, with potatoes and a rich gravy," I suggested. "This will make two state occasions in a row," I continued. "Don't forget Madeline and Helmut's engagement dinner on Friday."

Thursday, July 30

AFTER BREAKFAST MADELINE AND Helmut transferred all their luggage into the study so that Mona and Mackie could take the bedroom they had been using. Mona was painting her toenails in expectation of her husband and son's arrival. Lettie was helping Madeline and Helmut move bags. Jack and I drove to Balin-Mire and purchased a lovely pork roast for the evening's meal.

For lunch that afternoon we all headed down to the Marina. The crowd was local, mostly workingmen. There was a sink out back in the garden just outside the door where they could wash up, and Madame bantered good-naturedly with them, flirtatious and maternal at the same time. Like most of the village cafés at which we ate during our stay, the Marina had no menu, instead offering a plat du jour between twelve and two with carafes of an inexpensive but excellent local wine.

On this day Madame served a pork pâté followed by a creamy potato salad seasoned in a spicy rémoulade, and a beefsteak with frites. For dessert there was a choice of cheeses, chocolate mousse, or an almond custard, glazed across the top. All of it delivered at a price comparable to or even less expensive than an American restaurant.

We lingered over this satisfying meal for an hour or more, and still the majority of our fellow diners remained, socializing or sitting at the bar in front of the TV, with a beer and a last cigarette, to catch up on the soccer scores. What a difference, I thought, comparing this to workmen I had seen at home, rushing off to the convenience of the ever-popular "drive thru" or breaking for a quick half hour on-site to eat cold sandwiches driven up by a "catering" truck, served with coffee in disposable cups, before hustling back to the job.

You might ask, "A two-hour lunch! How does anything get done?" And it's certainly a fair question. I didn't have anything built while I was in France, but obviously, things got done. Houses were being constructed, cars got repaired, and streets were paved. How it got done, and how long it took, I have no idea. I suppose it's possible that if I lived here and hired a crew to work for me, I might go crazy with their schedule. But what I do know is, a two-hour lunch with a wonderful carafe of wine was definitely healthier—certainly physically and very possibly emotionally—than the previously mentioned alternatives. Again I had the sense that food and eating were prioritized with a tacit understanding of the great chef Brillat-Savarin's dictum: "Show me what you eat and I will tell you who you are." To prove it, I had just eaten a deliciously satisfying dinner and I was a very happy man.

～ ～ ～

AT THREE O'CLOCK, JACK opened the gate and I pulled the car into the street and tooted the horn. When Mona joined us, nicely dressed and wearing her new shoes, toenails painted a bright red, we headed off for the station at St.-Pierre-des-Corps. Mackie and Rory were coming in on the three-thirty train.

There would soon be eight of us. Truthfully I didn't want anything to change. I wanted these last two weeks to continue being as the two weeks before them had been, and, I confess, I was concerned about living with a fourteen-year-old. When you don't have teenage family members around, what you hear about adolescents is mostly what you see in the papers: rap music, big clothes, out-of-wedlock pregnancies, and 4-H clubs. I tried to imagine what I had been like at fourteen, recalling voices asking "Can't you keep yourself occupied for ten minutes?" I steeled myself for the change. When I voiced my concerns to Jack the night before, he, gifted with an inate rapport for both children and adolescents reassured me Rory would be a wonderful addition.

As it turned out, Jack was right. My misgivings regarding

Rory happily proved unfounded. From the beginning he was a considerate, enlivening presence and very funny. He dressed with a distinct sense of taste, but followed fashion from a judicious distance. He got off the train in a T-shirt (just a little oversized, I was relieved to note), and a shimmering green pair of those knee-length Michael Jordan shorts that were then *de rigueur* in America but still cutting-edge in Europe. With the requisite baseball hat, sunglasses, and sandals, the ensemble was very cool and an immediate hit. French teenagers approvingly checked him out. One day, later on during his stay, I used the shower off the study, which had become his bedroom and was amused by his collection of *petits nécessaires*, a multitude of bottles and tubes and containers of scrubs and paste and deodorants all lined up carefully in usable order.

As soon as we got to the house, Rory began exploring the caves, discovering more in his first five minutes than we had done in the whole two weeks we had been there. Mackie immediately fell in love with the house, and as an architect and excellent draftsman, he would make numerous, beautiful renderings of it in the weeks ahead.

We all sat around the terrace drinking wine before dinner, and even Rory was allowed a glass, since this was his first trip to France. Lettie set the table with the blue-and-white Limoges and, in the center, placed a low, white ironstone platter piled with flowers, fruits, and vegetables.

Dinner

Roast Pork in Red Wine with Carrots, Potatoes, and Green
  Beans
Pain de Campagne with Butter
Kiwi and Chocolate Ice Cream

I RUBBED THE PORK roast with olive oil, garlic, Dijon mustard, salt and pepper, and rolled it in flour, then browned it in the frying pan, put it into the baking dish, and roasted it uncovered at 450 degrees F. for twenty minutes. At that point I took the roast out, added a few bay leaves, herbes de Provence, and two good-size onions that I had sliced. I covered the dish, put it back into the oven, and turned the heat to 375 degrees. As it cooked, I scrubbed some carrots and potatoes while Rory picked a bowl of green beans (would the green beans ever end?).

About an hour later I added the potatoes, carrots (leaving them whole), and beans, sprinkling a little sugar on the carrots, and salt and pepper on the beans and potatoes. I poured two cups of red wine over the meat, re-covered it all, and let it bake for another hour.

The pork was done to perfection, cooked through, and the potatoes had browned in the wine and pork drippings, as had the carrots and beans. I removed the roast from the pan and drained off the grease, mixed two tablespoons of flour into a cup of red wine, and heating the juices in the baking dish over a low flame, I gradually added the wine and flour mixture, stirring constantly until the liquid became a rich brown gravy.

We ate the meal with bread and butter, and for dessert we had kiwi ice cream covered with a layer of dark chocolate ice cream. After dinner we took Mackie and Rory on a long walk, proudly showing the new arrivals the town in which, by this time, we had come to feel ourselves honorary residents.

Friday, July 31

WHEN I GOT BACK from the patisserie, Mackie was sitting out on the terrace drinking coffee.

"*Bonjour,*" he said. His French was much better than mine.

"*Bonjour,*" I replied. We sat and talked about his and Rory's stop in London, where they had stayed with Lettie's daughter—Rory's cousin—Agnes, who had squired them around the city's landmarks. In Paris they had stayed with Manuel and climbed the Eiffel Tower at midnight, avoiding the long lines of the day, and enjoying the beautiful lights of the city beneath them.

"You know, he's fourteen. This may be the last time he's going to want to do something with his parents," Mackie said.

≈ ≈ ≈

WHEN EVERYONE WAS UP and at the table, I began to organize the seating arrangement. I'm always disconcerted by families that have no fixed places for seating at the table. I grew up in a house in which, whatever seat you took when you were old enough to first sit at the table, was the one you kept for all of your life. When someone died you simply left their place vacant until a new family member arrived. Even now, when I go home, half a century after I first left, I sit in my assigned seat.

"Uh, no . . . *that's* where Jack sits," I told Rory. He moved toward Lettie's chair at the head of the table.

I shook my head no.

"Your aunt Lettie always sits there."

Rory stood back from the table, afraid to make a move.

"Helmut always sits there," I continued pointing, "and Madeline next to him. I sit here and"—pointing to the other chair—"Jack sits there, so let's put your father here, your mother next to him, three on each side, and you at the other end from your aunt Lettie."

Of course it occurred to me that people might be annoyed at being assigned seats, but I need to have order at the table. It's not neurotic. It's simply about not wanting to accept change.

∼ ∼ ∼

THIS WAS THE DAY of Madeline and Helmut's engagement celebration, and I needed to go into Balin-Mire to shop for something that would make a memorable feast. After breakfast, I pulled the car out alongside the terrace. "Anyone want to go shopping?" I shouted. To my surprise it was the four males who dashed for the car.

By this time, the employees at the ATAC had begun to recognize *les Americains*. Unlike the locals, who only spent a few francs buying enough food for a single day, each time we arrived, we loaded up our shopping cart and the bill would run into the hundreds, much to the checkout people's amused wonderment.

We divided into smaller units for maximum efficiency: Mackie and Helmut on a reconnaissance mission to the wine-and-bottled-water aisle; Rory pursuing breakfast Chex and chocolate; and Jack and I ferreting out a couple of rabbits. When Helmut pointed out some little green plums like the ones he and Madeline had eaten on their trip to the coast, I was inspired to make a green plum tart, and grabbed a premade butter pastry from the cold case. We were in and out of the market in a matter of minutes, and as we pulled back into the drive, I cried to the women of our group, who were sitting out on the terrace in the sun, "Home are the hunters, home from the hill."

"Did you, by chance, shoot any dish detergent?" Madeline called back.

~ ~ ~

LUNCH WAS SIMPLE: A little tomato and lettuce salad in a traditional vinegar and oil dressing with cheese and baguettes out on the terrace. From the distance of the fairgrounds, we could hear people setting up for the "Donkey Festival" scheduled to begin the next day: a weekend of music, food, games, and rides, with exhibition donkey races, donkey plowing contests, a donkey soccer playoff and a finale of fireworks on Sunday evening.

The Engagement Dinner

Roast Rabbit in Red Wine, Pleurettes, and Herbes de Provence
Green Beans Sautéed in Olive Oil and Garlic
Green Plum Custard Tart
1995 Domaine d'Oustric

THAT AFTERNOON, AS THE women began the ritual of dressing, I cut apart and dusted the two rabbits with flour and quickly browned them in a mix of olive oil and butter. Placing the pieces into a terra-cotta baking dish, I sprinkled them generously with herbes de Provence, covered them in sliced onions, and added about a pound and a half of sweet mushrooms, or pleurettes, then poured an entire fifth of red wine into the dish and covered it, setting it aside to marinate for a couple of hours. While Rory picked and snapped a bowl of beans, I began the tart with the green plums.

What a pleasure it was to simply unwrap a round of butter

pastry and lay it in the tart dish. Cutting the plums in halves, I removed the pits, laying the halves into the dish until it was filled. Then I whipped eight eggs with a cup of sugar and a little cinnamon and poured it over the plums. A half hour before we were to leave for the church, I set the rabbit and the tart into a 300 degree F. oven. Mackie had set the table, which was decorated with a dozen of the little crème caramel jars filled with flowers, and Lettie placed lace sachets of delicate candied almonds from the patisserie in front of each plate.

Madeline appeared in the white sleeveless blouse she had bought in Saumur and a long printed skirt with a shawl tied at the waist. She carried a small bouquet of roses, lavender, and dahlias. Helmut wore a white shirt and tie. When the rest of the gentlemen in the party were changed into slacks and shirts (which Lettie had kindly ironed for us), we all left for the church. As we made our way along the Rue de la Liberté, our neighbors, who had learned of the ceremony, came to their windows to watch us pass, wishing *"Bonne chance!"* and *"Felicitations!"* to the happy couple. Even Monsieur Deek came out to his sill and barked joyfully before returning to his pillow on the floor.

At the bottom of the hill, where the *rue* intersects Route D-7, the main road through town, the sidewalk narrows to a width of two feet, so that we were pressed into a single-file procession. Dressed in our finery, we looked like a parade of revelers, self-conscious but happy, as we made our way along the street past houses and shops to the church of St. Roche in the center of town.

Judging by the condition of this wonderful old edifice, the townspeople of Savonnieres were not as active a parish as their neighbors at nearby Balin-Mire, where the church was kept in much better order. Arriving with more than twenty minutes before the ceremony was to begin, we proceeded to examine points of interest within the building. Climbing the rickety spiral stairs, we found the choir loft; benches, director's podium, even the sheet music, were covered with a thick layer of dust, which must have been the accumulation of years.

We examined the uniformed statue of the patron, St. Roche. Taking him for a soldier, we wondered at the deep fissure in his thigh, which he indicated with one hand as, eyes turned upward in ecstatic contemplation, he gestured heavenward with the other. We were all charmed by his companion, a little dog looking like an ancestor of Monsieur Deek, sitting loyally at his side holding a loaf of bread in his mouth.

At precisely six-thirty the priest arrived. He was a tall man with a shaved head, dressed in a white-and-gold chasuble over a white cassock. When the introductions were completed, he invited us to the Virgin's Chapel at one side of the main altar. Candles had been lit and there was a bouquet of flowers beneath the statue.

Taking their places, Madeline and Helmut stood before the altar, the rest of us gathered in silence behind them.

The priest offered a French prayer of blessing and, laying

his hands over their heads, asked, in English, for a commitment to fulfill the engagement by marrying within a year.

They both agreed.

The priest blessed the betrothed couple, they kissed, and we all applauded.

"Now would be the time for some music," the priest said. "Do you know any songs?"

We stared dumbly. "None of us thought we were going to be asked to sing" seemed to describe the expression on all our faces. The only songs any of us could think of were a couple of French-Canadian folk tunes Lettie and Mona had been trying to teach us—one, about a cuckoo bird talking to an owl; the other, a raucous tavern round. When we informed the priest of our repertoire, he replied with a smile, "Well, perhaps no singing, then."

The ceremony concluded, we spent a little time chatting with the priest. He explained that St. Roche had, in fact, been a soldier. "That lesion on his leg," he added as an aside, "was higher, inside his groin, but for propriety's sake, the statue was fashioned with the wound placed a little lower."

Jack asked about the dog.

"Upon his return from battle, St. Roche found himself afflicted with the plague," the priest explained. "Fearful of contagion, the populace refused all contact with him, unwilling even to sell him bread. Starving, he prayed to the Virgin for aid, and in response, she sent the little dog, who fetched bread for him."

I would have preferred to be sent a cure rather than a trick dog, but this version made for a more interesting statue.

When, in the course of our conversation, Lettie mentioned our trip to Chenonceau, the priest told us that he had been stationed there for many years before coming to Savonnieres. Much as we had come to love this place, it did seem a step down from the swank little village of Chenonceau, though the manse behind the church looked comfortable enough. He was presently sharing it, the priest told us, with four Italians.

"It's a long story," he said, without a hint of anything.

We were of course intrigued, but none of us presumed to inquire further. Thanking the priest once again, we wished him a *bonsoir* and the eight of us walked back home up the hill to number 26 Rue de la Liberté for the betrothal feast.

When we arrived back at the house, the tart had finished baking and the rabbit was bubbling in the red wine, brown and tender. Again I quickly sautéed the green beans in olive oil (no one ever seemed to tire of the green beans, and besides, who was going to tell me if they did anyway? It's never wise to bite the hand that feeds you) and I called everyone to the table. We sat down to the feast, toasting the engaged couple with a bottle of Domaine d'Oustric '95. Rory won my heart by eating two helpings of the rabbit, and everyone wished there were two tarts, as we quickly finished off the one. After dinner we practiced our French songs and looked at a little television to check the weather. Tomorrow was the opening of the Donkey Festival. Tomorrow would also be Madeline and Helmut's last day here, but none of us wanted to think about that.

Saturday, August 1

ON THE FIRST WEEKEND in August, Savonnieres celebrates its annual Fête aux Ânes (Donkey Festival) in commemoration of the essential contribution made by this beast to the region's agrarian past.

On Friday afternoon there was already a considerable influx of people crowding the village, and by early Saturday morning an uninterrupted stream of people and cars was making its way along the road into the fairgrounds. There were games, exhibitions of crafts, plowing and pulling contests, a display of preindustrial farm implements, and of course, donkeys. The centerpiece of the festivities was a reenactment of the past, in which sacks of grain, drawn by donkey carts to the waterside, were loaded onto a *péniche*—a small square-rigged river barge—to be transported upstream to the old mill at Balin, ground, and returned as flour.

I had remained behind to finish some laundry when the others left the house that morning, and when I arrived at the fair sometime before noon, I found Lettie sketching happily amid a crowd of men costumed as bakers in knee-length white smocks, with long white stocking caps and flour dusted across their faces, who were waiting at the riverside for the returning boats.

We were invited by this congenial company to share the wine they were drinking and had already lifted our glasses in several toasts when the *péniche, La Saponaria*, suddenly came into view, turning at a bend in the river, flanked by two smaller boats, sails unfurled and horns blowing wildly, to herald the returning flour. When the boats had docked, the bakers transferred the milled grain back onto the donkey carts and we followed them to a place under the shade of the poplar grid at the center of the fairground. A brick, beehive oven, about four feet deep, with a high arched top and tall chimney, drawn here by donkey cart, had already been burning hot for more than an hour by the time the milled flour was returned. The bakers poured the flour into a huge bowl and added a simple mix of yeast, salt, and warm water to make a firm dough. They rolled the dough to a thickness of about an inch and cut it into small pieces to fashion biscuits, which they dusted lightly with flour. One of the bakers pushed the ashes to the sides and back of the oven, and the dough was baked for only a few minutes before a wonderful sheet of feathery light, slightly browned biscuits, each about the size of a silver dollar, emerged.

La fouée is what the bakers called them. The recipe purportedly originated in the Arab countries and seemed to me very much like the Italian foccacia—a leavened bread that rises only once before it is baked. The French took the recipe a step or two further, making delicate biscuits instead of simply baking the flat dough in loaves. The result is one of the most incredible little rolls I've ever eaten.

The bakers cut open the still-warm fouée and offered them freely to those of us watching, along with a choice of traditional fillings: snail butter (a mix of lemon, butter, and parsley); ground tuna; ground sardines; shredded pork (rillettes); goat cheese with chives; butter; chocolate; apricot preserves; and cassis jam.

When I told them that I was a chef, they insisted I have a taste of each filling and offered to send the recipe home to me. As this was all communicated in a combination of charades and French, I wasn't certain how much they understood of what I was saying, but after I had been home a month, the recipe arrived at the post office in Maine, sent by M. Graziani of La Poule Couasse. Anxious for readers to share in this culinary delight, I include the exact recipe as he has given it to me, along with another recipe for a dessert bread called *fouasse. Bonne chance!*

LA FOUÉE

200 grams de farine bise (dark flour)

60 grams d'eau (water)

1 cuillère à café de sel (salt)

20 grams de levain ou 1 cuillère à café de levure (yeast)

Souvent associe par erreur à la fouasse est une sorte de pain, lointain descendant du pain arabe, alors que la fouasse est une sorte de brioche. La fouée est un pain typiquement tourangeau, utilisé par les boulangers ou le possesseurs de fours banaux autrefois, pour "casser la croûte." Il est constitué d'un morceau de pâte prélevé sur la fournée et cuit sur la sole du four avant le pain, à four très chaud, en très peu de temps (3 ou 4 minutes).

My esteemed friend Dr. Barbara Hodgdon, professor of Renaissance literature at Drake University in Des Moines, Iowa, was kind enough to undertake the following translation.

Often associated erroneously with la fouasse, la fouée is a kind of "griddlecake," distantly descended from Arab bread, while la fouasse is a kind of brioche. La fouée is a typically tourangeau—that is, from the Tours region, or Touraine—bread, used by boulangers (bakers) or sometimes by those who own communal ovens, to casser la croûte—to test the crust for crispness (and the oven temperature)—and then eaten as a snack. It is made of a morsel of pastry cut into pieces in advance (to let rise) and baked on the hearthstone at a very high temperature, and for a short time—3 to 4 minutes.

Since the old ovens had no temperature gauges, bakers had to know when the oven was at the right heat for baking; these biscuits were their oven testers.

The recipe makes just a small amount, enough to test an old oven. The biscuits I ate at the fair were made with white flour and in a large enough batch to feed several people. I have converted the recipe.

8 1/4 cups all-purpose four
1 tablespoon salt
1 tablespoon dry yeast
3 cups very warm water from the tap

I make the dough by adding the salt and yeast to warm water, then mixing it into the flour. I knead it until it becomes an elastic dough, then roll it into a thickness of about an inch. Cutting the dough into rolls with a cookie cutter, I let them rise until they double in size. The rolls bake up perfectly.

Here is the recipe for the *fouasse*. This "bread" is almost a cake.

LA FOUASSE—OR FOUACE
250 grams pastry flour
200 grams wheat-meal flour
50 grams wheat germ
2 eggs

1 teaspoon salt

60 grams honey

20 grams yeast

4 tablespoons butter

100 grams hazelnuts

1 tablespoon orange water

6 strands saffron

First, knead together the flours, the wheat germ, the eggs, the salt, the honey, and the yeast. Then add the butter. Finally, incorporate the nuts, the orange water, saffron, and bake (cook) twenty minutes.

Other booths along the fairway offered goat sausages, andouillette (pork sausage), a North African spicy sausage called marguez, frites in a hot pepper puree, and plenty of red wine. Another niche presented a beautiful display of breads, croissants, and fruit tarts; while still one more offered croque-monsieur and croque-madame, or the ever-popular sandwich jambon, which I was happy enough to bypass.

At the back corner, where the fairgrounds are bounded by the river, donkeys were being shown and sold, tethered in a double row of small corrals, separated by a central aisle. There were mares, colts, and prize studs, of several different breeds, sizes, and colors, ranging from white to dark chocolate to a fuzzy silver gray, with various shades and patterns in between. Among them stood cuddly miniatures that looked like big stuffed toys, and the animal lover in Mona was drawn to an especially appealing one with dark eyes and snow-white fur. The little beast nuzzled up irresistibly, but when Mona hugged it, the others in the corral surged forward against the rope fence, attempting to stampede on her affection.

Moving away and continuing down the center aisle, Mona stopped from time to time to pet another and still another donkey. Halfway through the rows of tethers she stopped to hug a larger black animal with wild-looking eyes. Letting out a loud bray, he nuzzled up to her, and as she was hugging him, he—how do you say in your country?—became somewhat aroused. (Actually, with a donkey, there is no "somewhat" to his arousal.)

Turning a bright shade of pink and trying to avoid the stares of the very amused onlookers, Mona hurried down the aisle as the other donkeys, picking up on the moment and braying loudly, followed suit, their "curiosity" in full arousal. She had become a sort of "Helen of Savonnieres," launching not a thousand ships but a thousand donkey fantasies.

"Well," I smugly announced to her, "this, apparently, is a place in France that *I* can never come back to again."

Dinner

Sorrel and Spinach Salad
Herb-Roasted Chicken in White Wine
Oven Vegetables

THAT NIGHT FOR DINNER I quartered three chickens, salted, peppered, and sprinkled them with herbes de Provence, and put them into a hot 450 degree F. oven to brown for fifteen minutes. Then I poured on a couple of cups of white wine, covered them, and put them back into the oven, turning the heat down to about 350 degrees for forty-five minutes.

I then cut up a mixture of carrots, onions, potatoes, and mushrooms, tossed them in a few tablespoons of olive oil and a cup of red wine with salt, pepper, garlic, and fresh thyme, and placed them in a baking dish next to the chicken. Every now and again, for about forty-five minutes, I would stir them so they cooked more evenly.

Lettie made a little salad of fresh tomatoes, sorrel, and spinach from the garden, with an olive-oil-and-lemon dress-ing.

After dinner Madeline and Helmut began the sad chore of packing while the rest of us read or went for a walk, trying not to think too much about their departure.

Sunday, August 2

Breakfast

Baguette French Toast

WHEN THE ALARM WENT off at seven, I could smell coffee. Mackie was already setting the table.

The night before, I had cut a couple of stale baguettes into four-inch-thick pieces, whipped together six eggs, four cups of milk, a little salt, vanilla, and nutmeg, and set the bread in the mixture to soak overnight. By morning the bread pieces had soaked up the milk. I turned on the oven to 400 degrees F. and placed the hunks of baguette on a buttered cookie sheet. I baked the bread until they puffed up, and turned golden—

about fifteen to twenty minutes. We ate them with butter and pure maple syrup.

After breakfast we helped Madeline and Helmut carry their luggage out to the car. The morning, bright and warm, was tinged with sadness. Everyone kissed good-bye, Helmut and Madeline took a last look at the house and the garden, and Mona and I drove them out through the gate and on to the station at St.-Pierre-des-Corps for the 10:27 TGV (fast train) to Paris.

The platform was crowded. When the train arrived, there was a great push of people, shoving and tossing their luggage before them to get on board. Madeline and Helmut waited until they were the last two passengers to get on. Friends from childhood, Mona and Madeline wept as they parted. We watched Helmut and Madeline through the windows, following their progress through the coach to their seats, finally waving our last good-byes as the train slowly pulled away. I knew that I would be seeing them again in a couple of weeks, but I was also aware that time and events pass only once, and can never be exactly the same again. Still I hoped that what we had all shared and become together in this bright interlude might somehow not vanish completely.

Lunch

Scrambled Eggs with Toasted Baguette and Butter

IT WAS ALMOST NOON before we got back, and hungry again, I made a lunch of scrambled eggs with toast. Whipping a dozen eggs with a couple of containers of petit suisse, I added salt and fresh ground black pepper. I melted a great hunk of butter in the frying pan, heated it until it began to sizzle, and then poured the eggs into the butter, holding the pan over the flame and shaking it continuously until the eggs were cooked. If you've never done this, it's a great way to fry an egg and it makes your pan easy to clean. Rory cut a baguette on the angle into long thin slices and toasted them under the broiler. We ate them with butter, along with the eggs, and drank another pot of coffee. The mood was just slightly off center.

That afternoon, Jack and I returned for a second visit to the château of Villandry. Before entering, we stopped for a cup of coffee at the café outside the gates. Jack ordered a cassis crepe and I had a slice of apricot tart. My appetite had become voracious. Maybe I was just trying to fill the empty space left by Helmut and Madeline's departure.

Afterward, we explored the wooded paths on the elevations overlooking the gardens, which were relatively empty that afternoon, the usual crowds having been drawn away by the local festivities. Beneath us, the bright colors of the flowers shimmered and glowed against the solid greens of the parterred hedges. In the village beyond the walls of the château, the beautiful Norman church stood like an anchor in the stream of time, while across the river a herd of black-and-white cows grazed placidly in their green valley—a vision of peace, making us both grateful to have found ourselves the recipients of so much pleasure.

~ ~ ~

SINCE THERE WAS NO one there when we got back to the house, we returned to the fairgrounds, arriving at halftime of the donkey soccer play-offs. On a stage at the end of the soccer field, "les Nouvelles Femmes," a troupe of long-legged, pretty cheerleaders, danced and lip-synched to a Spice Girls song. When the act was finished, they moved off to the sidelines and the mock game resumed.

In silly costumes, the "Brazilian" and "French" teams kicked an enormous soccer ball around the field from donkeyback. When one of France's donkeys mounted a Brazilian donkey, the crowd jumped to its feet, cheering as the referee, arms waving wildly, called "Foul!"

The winning goal for the French actually conked a Nouvelle Femme on the head, knocking her from the fence behind the goal where she had been sitting. Legs in the air, blond hair flying, she tumbled to the ground. Mortified, the young lady got up, patted her hair, forced a smile, and pulled herself back up onto the fence. The crowd roared in the bleachers and rose to a standing ovation as the player who kicked the winning goal took a grand and flourishing bow. The French had won again. *Vive la France!*

Dinner

Cold Rabbit
Chèvre and Camembert Fouée Sandwiches
Chocolate–Passion Fruit Ice Cream
Chocolate-Pistachio Ice Cream

THAT NIGHT WE FINISHED the leftover rabbit from Helmut and Madeline's engagement dinner with little Camembert and goat-cheese sandwiches made from a bag of the foueé that Mona had brought back from the fair. On the way home from Villandry that afternoon, I had picked up two quarts of ice cream from the patisserie: chocolate–passion fruit and chocolate-pistachio, which we ate while relaxing out on the terrace together, watching the sun set and the little bats, who emerged from the caves each evening, fly about in the fading light of the garden.

At the back of the laundry was a heavy door and iron gate, which opened onto a flight of stone stairs that took you up the hill above the caves. There was a view overlooking the river valley and the fairgrounds. It was dark when we unlocked the back door to the stairs, and ascending to the top, we settled ourselves down to watch the fireworks.

Hundreds of cars were parked over the fields below us, and by ten o'clock, at long last, the display commenced. It was remarkable to be sitting on a hillside in France watching a fireworks display, applauding the rockets' sprays of colored fire flying through the night sky, hearing the shouts and the music of the band in the distance. When the last booming rockets of the finale were fading away, a great cheer rose up from the fairgrounds. Long past midnight I could still hear the merrymaking. Crowds of people singing Queen's "We Are the Champions" in English could be heard above the honking of cars as they made their way from the fields to the highway. The fairgoers, like celebrants everywhere, seemed to want to squeeze one final moment from the festivities. Just before dozing off, I heard the bells from St. Roche strike three, and in the distance, the final tipsy strains of "We Are the Champions" from what surely must have been the end of the celebrants straggling home.

Breakfast

Toasted Raisin Bread with Sautéed Fruit

THAT MORNING I BOUGHT a raisin bread. It was very unlike the raisin bread I was accustomed to. It was made from a dark dough, a sort of cross between a very coarse wheat and a rye. The raisins were plump, but the loaf wasn't rolled with cinnamon and sugar like our raisin bread. I cut thin slices to lie under the broiler for toast.

I had sautéed equal amounts of sliced pears and apples in butter, sugar, vanilla, and cinnamon. When the bread was toasted, I ladled the cooked fruit over it and reassigned places around the table, Mackie and Rory taking over the vacancies left by Madeline and Helmut. We hoped their return flight was better than the one that had brought them here.

≈ ≈ ≈

LETTIE'S DAUGHTER, AGNES, WAS arriving from London the next evening. She would be celebrating her thirtieth birthday with us the following Monday. It was another excuse for a feast. Lettie and I discussed the different possibilities for a menu, finally settling on duck breast in a sauce of crème de cassis.

"I'll even do a chartreuse of vegetables," I offered.

A chartreuse of vegetables is a freestanding crown of nine vegetables—invented by the Chartreuse monks, who were vegetarians. It makes a spectacular presentation with a mix of carrots, string beans, zucchini, summer squash, peas, potatoes, cabbage, brussels sprouts, and cauliflower. I had discovered the recipe thirty years ago and was so impressed that I decided to try it. From the very first effort, it never failed.

"We can go to that patisserie in Balin-Mire," Mona suggested, jumping in excitedly. "They have beautiful whipped-cream cakes." The plans were beginning to develop into a full-fledged celebration.

Jack had the idea of making crowns of laurel with florist's wire and construction-paper leaves, and we made the necessity of obtaining the materials an excuse for a trip into Tours.

Rory and Mackie joined Jack and me. Rory had discovered the existence of a cyber café in Tours while surfing his computer at home, and he and Mackie were anxious to check it out. Later that afternoon we all met for a drink before the train ride home.

The cyber café had been somewhat disappointing, but Rory had found another point of interest he was anxious to share. While walking through the city he had spotted a Coke machine in front of a department store and returned with a can; the conversation, though not verbatim, went something like this:

"Hey guys! This can of Coke was only ten francs and I got fourteen ounces, but did you know when we buy a bottle of it in the café in Savonnieres you only get twelve ounces and it's thirteen francs? And at the train station you can get a can but it's twelve francs. We should stock up on cans from the machine at the department store—we could save a fortune."

If the practicality of his proposal was questionable, this precision of calculation was typical of a fourteen-year-old who had been successfully playing the stock market with his weekly allowance.

When I once, offhandedly, suggested that a destination was only a five-minute walk, he reflexively corrected me. "Oh no, it's at least a twelve- to fifteen-minute walk." Of course he was right. The walk took about fifteen minutes.

"Are you six years old or twenty?" I overheard Jack asking him once.

Being fourteen is like that.

When Rory first arrived, he was like a little kid, excitedly chasing through the caves and exploring every inch of the compound; but when we went swimming in the Cher, where some of the women sunbathed topless, he arranged the blanket on the downward swoop of the bank, and relaxing there, chin propped on his hands, hat and sunglasses covering his eyes, took in the scene. In recounting the experience later, he giggled and blushed.

"The French revere breasts so much they even named a town after one of them," I told him. "Brest. It's somewhere on the coast, I think."

He, of course, thought I was a lunatic.

His affection for his parents was remarkable and, in retrospect, completely unlike my own adolescence. One afternoon I came across him and his father in the living room. The two of them were reading together, Rory leaning on Mackie's shoulder, engrossed in a book, looking completely secure and happy. I envied the closeness of a relationship I had never known as a son and would never know as a father.

≈ ≈ ≈

BACK AT THE HOUSE that afternoon, Jack set everyone about the task of making the paper wreaths for the upcoming birthday party. While they cut and snipped and twisted the paper into bright leaves, I began dinner.

Dinner

Vegetarian Risotto

IN THE REFRIGERATOR WERE three small chickens I had gotten on sale some days earlier and forgotten. Unwrapping them now, I noticed they had a slight smell. Washing them under cold water didn't seem to help.

"Do you think these smell okay?" I asked. Lettie stuck her nose into the cavity of one of the chickens. "Oh! I think this is bad. I don't think we should eat it."

Mona put her scissors down, walked over to the sink, and buried her nose in the cavity, then into the other two birds. "No! Not good—none of them. We'll get ptomaine. I don't want to have to go next door again."

Wrapping the chicken in plastic, I took them out to the garbage and returned to the kitchen to see what else might be in the larder.

Perusing the contents of the refrigerator, I found a few mushrooms, a couple of leeks, two red peppers, and a lone zucchini. In the cupboard was a bag of rice. I placed the red peppers over the open gas jet and roasted them until they were black, then peeled them. In a frying pan I heated olive oil and added the uncooked rice to brown, shaking the pan from time to time to keep it from burning. I poured two cups of red wine into a pot with two cups of water and brought the mix to a boil while I chopped the zucchini, mushrooms, and leeks, four red ripe tomatoes, and the peppers. When the rice was browned, I added the vegetables and the boiling wine-water mixture to the pan and seasoned it with fresh thyme, fresh marjoram, salt and pepper, and the juice of two lemons. There were bits and pieces of the hard Italian cheese, a couple of soft cheeses that had long since lost their original packaging and names, and a hunk of goat cheese, all of which I ground together in the food processor then sprinkled over the rice. I covered the mixture and turned it down low for about fifteen minutes until the rice was cooked.

A lovely vegetarian risotto.

Clearing away the yellow and green paper, wire, scissors, and completed wreaths, we set the table and sat down to eat, discussing the party for Agnes as we dined. After dinner, when the dishes had been washed and put away, everyone went back to making wreaths. They had to be finished by tonight and hidden away, since Agnes was arriving the next afternoon.

While the others resumed their work on the party hats, I took a long walk on the road through the sunflower fields. The poplar grove at the fairgrounds and the expanse of mown grass around where the Donkey Festival had been was again empty of people. No rides, no donkeys or bakers, only this space of perfect solitude.

The evening light spread a glowing golden color across the

sunflowers, and I had the inexplicable feeling that the flowers were pleased to see me. If the flirtations I had felt when we first arrived had led to "love's first kiss" that morning I sat by myself on the terrace drinking coffee and listening to music, these past two and a half weeks had turned into a full-fledged love affair with France. Looking around me to be certain I was alone, I spoke to the field of sunflowers, thanking them for being there, telling them what a magnificent place this was, and how grateful I was to be here. I was certain that they not only heard and understood, but that, if it had been possible, they would have reached out to enfold me in their color.

Tuesday, August 4

AFTER OUR USUAL BREAKFAST of baguettes and croissants, I drove to the ATAC in Balin-Mire. I had already picked up a dozen beautiful apples (for another tart), some potatoes, carrots, and mushrooms when I stopped at the meat counter to order turkey cutlets—this time enough for seven, the number Agnes's arrival that afternoon would make us.

"Mousse de canard?" I asked as I took the cutlets the butcher had wrapped up in white paper for me. The man indicated a cold case back in produce. Delighted to have made myself understood, I strolled off, nodding gracious *bonjours* to other shoppers. I picked up the container and continued adding some wine to the cart, a bottle of creme de cassis, more sparkling water, and of course, a variety of chocolate

bars. I felt so confident shopping alone, I assumed people thought I was a native.

Then I hit the checkout counter.

"*Le prix?*" the young lady asked, holding up the *mousse de canard.* I understood I was being asked a question, but beyond that I had no idea what she was saying. Stunned out of my self-confidence, I stared blankly. The woman stared back and we both began to laugh. "*Je ne parle pas français,*" I admitted, embarrassed. The man in line behind me moved off to another checkout while the young lady called to someone from produce for a price check. As we waited I began to bag my other purchases.

It is a remarkable experience not being able to speak or understand the language in a foreign land. You are suddenly reduced to pointing and making sounds as though you've become a child who hasn't yet learned to talk. Both the checkout lady and I, neither speaking the other's tongue, in that instant of nonverbal recognition, reclaimed a moment of innocence.

The price check completed and the bags packed, the check-out lady and I exchanged a very cordial nod, both grinning from ear to ear as I headed for the car and she turned to help the next customer.

Dinner

Turkey Cutlets with a Sorrel Breading in a Champagne and Leek Cream Sauce

Oven-Roasted Vegetables

Fresh Tomatoes in a Lemon Dressing

Apple Tart with Vanilla and Cinnamon

AGNES WAS ARRIVING ON the late-afternoon TGV, and while Mack and Lettie drove to the station at Tours to meet her, I began dinner.

I made some bread crumbs by grinding leftover pieces of baguettes with a handful of fresh sorrel. I dipped the turkey cutlets into a mixture of crème fraîche whipped with an egg, then rolled them into the sorrel breading, and gently sautéed them in an equal mix of butter and olive oil—enough to cover the bottom of the pan an eighth of an inch. Once the cutlets were browned on both sides, I transferred them into a terra-cotta baking dish, doused them with a quarter bottle of flat champagne (I couldn't bring myself to throw out even flat French champagne), covered them, and slipped the pan into a 400 degree F. oven.

I made a mixture of carrots, potatoes, onions, and string beans in olive oil seasoned with fresh rosemary, basil, thyme, garlic, salt, and pepper, and put it into a baking dish, uncovered, to cook with the turkey. While it was all baking I went to the garden and gathered a colander full of young leeks, which I chopped and washed and set aside. In a saucepan I made a roux with a quarter pound of butter and a cup of flour, added one cup of white wine and three cups of light cream, some salt, pepper, and a little nutmeg, stirring continuously until it came to a boil and began to thicken. Then I added the leeks, turned the heat down, and let it simmer. When the turkey was done—it took just about a half hour—I took the pan out of the oven, drained off the juices, and added them to the leek sauce. I let the sauce simmer for a couple of minutes, poured it over the cutlets, turned the heat down to 350 degrees, and let them simmer in the oven until the vegetables were done, another fifteen to twenty minutes.

It was almost two hours since Lettie and Mack had left for the station. Mona had become concerned.

"You don't think anything has happened, do you?" she asked apprehensively. The rest of us assured her that nothing had happened. Just as Lettie walked out onto the terrace to watch for them, we heard the horn at the gate. They had arrived. Mackie explained that he had taken a wrong turn coming through the traffic circle and was on his way to Provence before they realized what had happened.

Agnes was lovely. Long blond hair with the same bright look in her eyes as her mother. She was Rory's only cousin from Mona's side of the family and he clearly adored her, cozying up next to her while she sipped a glass of wine and talked about her travels.

Agnes had been born when Lettie was still in college, and had spent her early years in her grandfather's house in New Hampshire before moving to Toledo after her mother's marriage. As an adolescent, she had found summer employment as an au pair in Switzerland and France, an experience from which she derived a love of travel. Following high school, she had enlisted in the army, where she earned a degree in business administration. After the service, she had won a position in a relief organization of the UN that worked to stimulate small business entrepreneurship. She had worked in Poland and Armenia. In Poland, she told us, she had been involved in opening a restaurant, initially even undertaking some of the cooking.

"They loved the food," she told us proudly. "There were no other restaurants in town. Within a week we were so busy it was hard to handle it all."

She was presently living in London, where she was working on a doctoral degree in business administration.

While we got aquainted Lettie made a salad of the fresh tomatoes with a dressing of basil, corn oil, salt, pepper, and lemon juice. A perfect complement to the dinner. I had also made an apple tart with a round of the butter pastry I had bought in the market.

I peeled and cored eight apples, cut them in half, then sliced each half into eight thin pieces and laid them in the pastry so that the slices looked like apple halves. When the tart shell was filled, I mixed together a half cup of sugar, a stick of butter, a tablespoon of cinnamon, and three table-spoons of vanilla, spread this mixture over the apples, painted the edges of the crust with a mix of egg yolk and two table-spoons of water, then put it into a 325 degree F. oven and let it bake for about an hour until the sugar caramelized over the apples. Cinnamon, apples, butter, sugar, and vanilla make a simple and wonderful combination of flavors. One half cup of sugar seems about perfect for any of the fruit tarts, but of course it really depends on the baker's taste.

Vanilla and cinnamon are two of the most common and popular flavorings. Throughout my career I had reached for the most improbable combinations I could conjure, bypassing the traditional in favor of any blending of food that would prove my iconoclasm: parsnips in oranges, curry, and apricot brandy; swordfish steaks in coffee brandy and soured cream; chocolate-lavender ice cream; coconut cream soup. Like a lot of chefs, I would hit on a spice, an herb, or new ingredient and then use it in as many ways and combinations I could imag-ine until I felt every possibility had been exhausted. While I continue to applaud that approach, I have begun to work backward, looking to return that "iconoclastic" taste to the most simple of dishes. Now I was stretching the ordinary just to see, once again, what that taste could be. Perhaps looking for another culinary jumping-off place.

Wednesday, August 5

MACKIE THOUGHT IT WOULD be a good experience for Rory to take the daily trip to the patisserie that morning. Stuffing a fifty-franc note into his shirt pocket, his father told him, "You need to make certain you get a receipt."

"And be careful crossing the street," I added.

"Make sure the bread is fresh," Mackie cautioned.

"And try not to lose the fifty francs," I chided. "And do you think you could also stop at the grocery and get a container of milk?"

Donning his hat and sunglasses, Rory replied, "Yes, Buddy (my familial nickname), I think I could do that," with that hint of the impatience young people assume when being instructed by their elders.

"*Lait* is the word for 'milk'!" I yelled after him, his father and I chuckling.

A short time later he returned unscathed, milk and breakfast in hand, correct change and even a receipt in his pocket. When I told him how impressed I was with his success, I got one of those "Oh, God, what do you think I am!" looks.

~ ~ ~

A FEW DAYS EARLIER, we had determined that we would take Agnes out to eat at a restaurant that was a little more upscale than the local café and decided to have lunch at a place just out of town called Les Cèdres. The green book had given it a four-star rating but warned that it was pricey. We didn't care.

We arrived at Les Cèdres and were greeted by a tall, slender woman with hennaed hair, wearing a silk blouse, a pair of black slacks and high heels. She led us to a corner table and we ordered a bottle of wine and perused the menu. There was a *prix fixe* of 115 francs (which at the time was about twenty dollars) for the complete lunch.

Rory didn't feel like eating a four-course lunch, so he ordered an omelet jambon à la carte with a glass of milk.

My meal began with a salad made with three different kinds of lettuce served in a simple but exquisitely delicious vinegar-and-oil dressing. We shared appetizers of pâtés, quiche, crudités, and mousse de fois gras, along with warm bread from the oven. All of it excellent. For the main course, Lettie and Jack had venison in a dark and winy reduction sauce that contained shallots and was generously seasoned with herbes de Provence. Mackie and Agnes ordered ham-and-spinach-filled crepes covered with a most wonderful sherried cream sauce that contained finely chopped pieces of ham, peppers, and onions. Mona and I had pheasant, also in a dark sauce, with currants along with the juices from the roasted bird. Each of the dishes was served with green beans and a baked potato stuffed with Gruyère. We had not been misled. The food was superior. The chef, Jean-Pierre Gessier, is truly an artist. All of it had been memorable. We drank a bottle of the restaurant's own red wine with dinner, and for dessert had an apricot tart, with a dish of vanilla ice cream for Rory.

Dinner

Turkey Salade Niçoise

IT WAS LATE INTO the evening before any of us felt like eating again. I took the leftover turkey, added some fresh string beans and what was left of the roasted vegetables from the night before, and made a sort of salade niçoise (*sans* the tuna, olives, anchovies, lettuce, tomatoes, and eggs), with a little balsamic vinegar and olive oil. Whatever you want to call it, it was just what we wanted to eat after the enormous lunch at Les Cèdres.

Thursday, August 6

THIS WAS THE DAY JACK and I selected for an excursion to Paris. The temperature at eight in the morning was already approaching ninety degrees.

"You're not going dressed like that, are you?" Lettie asked when we appeared at breakfast that morning wearing shorts and T-shirts.

"No?" Jack asked doubtfully.

"You don't want to look like a couple of bumpkins in Paris, do you?" Mona asked.

"You should dress," Lettie insisted. "Wear something nice."

And so, after finishing our croissants and coffee, we quickly changed into slacks and cotton shirts with collars before Mackie drove us off to the station at St.-Pierre-des-Corps for the ten-thirty TGV to Paris.

We arrived at Montparnasse at eleven-thirty. It was a little overwhelming at first, after the weeks in tiny Savonnieres, to find ourselves in a major metropolis, and we stopped for a second cup of coffee at the station to collect ourselves.

En route through Paris to Savonnieres, Mackie and Rory had visited the Musée d'Orsay, and on their recommendation, we had decided to visit it as well. We caught the métro and, following Mackie's directions, ascended to the street two stops later. It was a beautiful clear morning but already quite warm. Luckily the museum was only a short walk away.

Originally built as a train station for the great exposition of 1900, the Orsay houses a premier collection of sculpture, paintings, and artifacts produced between the years 1848 to 1914, including the originals of many of the most frequently reproduced images of the modern era. The museum was relatively empty when we arrived, but by the time we made our way to the galleries on the top floor, where we found van Gogh's yellow-and-blue bedroom hanging alongside one of Cézanne's mysterious bathing scenes, the crowd had become a distraction. We watched as a middle-aged tourist in combat fatigues, apparently filming a video to be viewed at some later time in the privacy of his "media room," scanned the four walls with his camcorder and abruptly marched on to repeat the procedure in the rooms beyond. An Asian woman, bowing a thousand obsequious apologies for the intrusion, positioned herself directly between us and a second Cézanne, a still life of flowers in a blue vase. We moved on to another painting, and within moments the same woman, again bobbing up and down and smiling in apology, placed herself between us and it.

"Should we get some lunch?" I suggested as a pleasant alternative to an untoward situation. Jack grinned and we headed for the café, which is also located on the top floor, looking out onto a balcony with a view across the Seine to Sacré-Coeur in Montmartre. The food was amazingly good, especially considering the numbers being fed, and reasonably priced—a little more than Tours but quite manageable. I had an open-faced sandwich of smoked trout and smoked salmon on slices of toasted baguette with crème fraîche mixed with chives and a wonderful mayonnaise served with a fresh green salad. Jack ordered a sandwich jambon (of which he, at least, seemed never to tire) and a bottle of beer.

After lunch, we made our way into a small darkened room given over to a display of works by the Symbolist painter Odilon Redon. The paintings hung in glass cases, their jewel-like colors illuminated by pinspots. In the next room we found some early works of Gauguin hanging beside the Pointillist Signac.

By this time we decided that we had digested our limit and were making our way to the exit when we passed a sign for an exhibit of American works. Curious to see what might be included, we found ourselves directed into an enormous room at the corner of the building. Originally the ballroom of the station's hotel, it was fantastically ornate, after the fashion of a "cottage" at Newport. I don't recall any of the paintings or much of the sculpture—mostly figures of women, overheavy and lugubrious looking for my tastes, with the notable exception of an angel of Saint-Gaudens in bas-relief on bronze, perhaps seven feet high. She looked like a young Katharine Hepburn, dressed in a Grecian tunic, her arms lifted straight out in cruciform.

I had long known Saint-Gaudens's memorial to Captain Shaw and his African-American regiment that sits across from the state house on the Boston Common, and I had visited Saint-Gaudens's house and studio in Cornish, New Hampshire. There I had seen preliminary castings for the Adams Memorial at Rock Creek Cemetery in Washington, D.C. On the desk in his study there was a miniature copy of the beautiful *Diana*—now at Philadelphia's Museum of Art—initially perched *en pointe* at the tip of the cupola of the original Madison Square Garden. I remembered the striding Lady Liberty on the silver dollar of his design, which was very much like this angel at the Orsay. Surrounded by a collection that was not representative of the best of American art, the angel stood apart, staring full-face boldly forward like a reproach to the too-florid charms of the more languid beauties surrounding her.

By the time we left the museum, it was midafternoon and terrifically hot—the second day of a heat wave that was to continue unabated until the middle of our final week. We couldn't help but notice that we appeared to be the only men in the entire city not dressed in shorts.

Following the river along the Quai Anatole France, we crossed to the Place de la Concorde and entered the Tuileries Gardens, stopping to admire the long sweep of the avenue. The great hedges of the pleached chestnuts, which must be spectacular in bloom, were already beginning to brown and drop their first leaves. Recently cleaned, the obelisk shone in the hot sun, thrusting itself up directly through the center of the distant Arc de Triomphe.

At the Louvre, the crowds swarmed around Pei's pyramid, so that even if we'd had the appetite for looking at more paintings we might have been discouraged. From the Louvre we made our way back across the river, walking along the cobblestone embankment as far as the Île de la Cité, the island that stands in the middle of the Seine and supports Notre Dame. It was wonderful to step down out of the city into that place of water and stone with its succession of beautiful bridges. People fished or sat talking; lovers, holding hands, passed us oblivious to anything but themselves. We passed small barges that were houseboats, the smell of food cooking enticing us to come closer. A woman was hanging laundry on the roof of her boat.

Occasional flights of age-old granite steps led down into the water, evoking fantasies of kings and their retinue alighting from boats. Nothing makes you feel Paris more than walking along the Seine.

Jack was anxious to visit Shakespeare and Company, the legendary bookstore of expatriot English-speaking literati since the 1920s. The store, a series of little rooms and passageways, is crammed with books. Students sat cramped into corners, noses buried in some tattered tome, or like us, browsed idly, stopping occasionally to examine a title where James Baldwin or Tennessee Williams might have once stood perusing a copy of André Gide's journals. Jack purchased a paperback copy of Auden's *The Dyer's Hand and Other Essays* and Daudet's *Letters from My Windmill* and we made our way back through the Latin Quarter.

We passed by the Hôtel la Louisianne, where I had stayed fifteen years before in the midst of a disintegrating love affair. Fifteen years ago you could get a double with breakfast for thirty dollars. Now the same accommodations went for seventy dollars. The charcuterie nearby, where I had eaten then, had been sold to some Asian people—and though the food was no longer French, the offerings seen in the window were as elegant as before.

It was sad and strange to return to this scene. It seemed as if an unhappy portion of me had been preserved and was lingering here still, unchanged by all the intervening years. I recalled so many things, but now with a poignant detachment from all the remorse of those unhappy days.

The remainder of the hours left to us were spent strolling along the embankment beside the river. Finally, exhausted, we dropped into a corner café someplace in the neighborhood of the Eiffel Tower, both of us parched from the heat. The prices were astonishing. When we figured out the exchange rate, we realized that for two medium-sized Badouits (sparkling water) we had paid seven dollars and fifty cents a glass. But the waiter was so attractive and kind, it was impossible to feel annoyed. We asked him how to get back to the station at Montparnasse. He spoke almost no English, but deliberate and careful with his pronunciation as he was, even we had little trouble following him.

"Traversez le pont . . . à gauche, le métro." (Cross the bridge . . . on your left is the subway.)

We thanked him and started on our way a bit uneasily, as there was now little time left for any mis-navigations if we hoped to make our train home. Studying the map at the métro, we realized that it was necessary to switch trains, but we managed this without mishap and arrived with time to spare, leaving on the 7:30 P.M. TGV direct to St.-Pierre-des-Corps.

With Jack dozing in the seat opposite, I watched the countryside speeding past. It was hard to believe we were traveling a hundred and thirty miles per hour—the ride was so comfortable and smooth. Because of this speed, the tracks had been laid out to avoid the towns and villages as much as possible. We were passing through an expanse of the farthest fields, their recently cut stubble parched yellow and brown after the intense heat of the afternoon, the houses and barns off at a distance, miles away, with green-wooded hills behind them.

Mona and Mackie were waiting at the station when we arrived. Agnes had cooked a fine dinner for us. There was a leek-and-petit-suisse quiche made with egg yolks and Emmenthal cheese in a puff pastry, and a lentil-and-hazelnut salad in a simple olive-oil-and-vinegar dressing. Like her mother, Agnes was a superb cook.

After supper we all relaxed together on the terrace, discussing our trip to Paris and their excursion to Amboise, where they had visited Clos Luce, the house where Leonardo da Vinci had died.

AFTER BREAKFAST THAT MORNING, Jack and I set off on a hike upriver to the mill. At the green-doored farmhouse, where the road turned away from the river into the sunflower fields, a little dog silently lifted his snout and beat a listless greeting with his tail. It was a hot day for walking, but we continued, following along the water where the road became a rutted lane, a strip of rough sod running down the center. Somewhere along the way we crossed the line between Savonnieres and the town of Balin, where the mill is located. The countryside took on a more remote feeling. The woods opened into a large mowed field dotted with rolled bales of hay. Farther along, the trees again closed around us, opening a quarter of a mile later into more fields. Save for an untenanted stone house and barn with burnt-orange roofs of clay tiles, the fields were empty and we could see across to green-and-blue hills on the other side of the valley.

Sometime long after one o'clock, we arrived at the mill. Even on this blazing day it was a refreshing sight reflected in the water, its great wooden wheel immobile. A crescent-shaped sandbar formed a deep pool before it. We were amused to find two men fishing together in nonchalant indifference to a sign that prohibited fishing nailed into the tree trunk against which one of them stood resting.

From behind the hedge of the garden of what appeared to be the mill owner's house, a little dog barked frantically as we passed. The road had turned to pavement again and took us by the new electric-powered mill and over a bridge spanning a rush-choked moat that separated the mill yard from the modest houses of the neighborhood beyond. In French fashion, the gardens were clearly delineated according to function by low boxwood or perhaps lavender hedges: an area of grass or pavement for sitting and dining immediately outside the house; a mixed plot of roses and vegetables in neat rows; and a toolshed set back in one corner. There was an orderly sameness to the design, yet individuality was beautifully apparent with each person's choice of flowers, shed, and vegetables.

Eventually, we arrived at the main road and were happy to find ourselves at the café where Lettie, Madeline, Mona, and I had eaten lunch so perilously close to the oncoming traffic that first day following Madeline's arrival. Coming from the riverside, we now discovered a dining pavilion in the garden behind and gratefully took a table in its shade.

Having delivered lunches to another party, the waitress disappeared into the café without acknowledgment of our arrival. After what seemed an inordinate wait, I went in to see about ordering some lunch.

The proprietor waved his hands. *"Ferme!"* he insisted.

I looked at the clock. It was past two. *"Possible . . . sandwich jambon . . . pour deux, s'il vous plaît?"*

He nodded. *"Oui."*

"Une bière et une Coca?"

"Oui."

"Merci, monsieur."

Back outside, I told Jack, "I don't think this guy likes Americans."

"Why? What makes you say that?" he asked, leaning back and stretching his legs.

"It's only a few minutes past two. He could have given us lunch."

"Well," Jack observed judiciously, "when they say twelve to two, that's what they mean."

"Do you think everyone in France is eating a ham sandwich?"

"They are if it's after two o'clock," he replied.

The man appeared with our order. The cold drinks in the hot afternoon were like an elixir and the sandwich jambons deliciously revived our strength. Looking out across the fields, we sat talking for a long time about France and about ourselves, and for the first time in all the years I had known him, Jack said, "You know, I think I'll be published soon." It was as though the serenity and beauty of this time away in France had worked some subtle magic that brought a vision of change to all of us.

When we got back, the house was empty, but before leaving, the others had closed the windows and pulled all the draperies, and the thick stone walls still held in the cooler air of the morning. Exhausted from our long walk, we read and dozed until the four of them returned late that afternoon with a box of magnificent peaches, every one large and perfect, the color a Titian red, with a green leaf or two still caught at the stems. Their aroma filled the air; they were perfectly ripe. Four were already missing from the flat. I grabbed one and bit into it. It was everything I had remembered a seasoned peach to be—sweet, juicy, and as fulfilling to the taste buds as the golden color of the flesh was to the eye.

Agnes had brought a bottle of Pimms No. 1 for a "Pimms Cup," the original gin sling made from a mixture of Pimms with ginger ale or club soda, flavored with mint and served over ice with lemon, orange, and cucumber rinds.

Dinner

Potato Salad in a Raspberry Honey Dressing
Peach Custard Tart

WHILE THE REST OF the group was enjoying this odd cocktail out on the terrace, Lettie put together a cold salad of potatoes, peppers, and peas in a dressing of raspberry vinegar sweetened with honey (I could still taste goat), which she served with a baguette cut into large croutons, spread with butter, Parmesan, and fresh basil, and toasted under the broiler.

Meanwhile, I had begun a peach tart for dessert. I buttered the dish, unwrapped a puff-pastry round, and carefully laid it in. Then I cut six peaches in halves, removed the pits, and scraped away any of the tough parts from around where the pits had been. I sliced each half into six thin pieces and began overlapping them in a circle until the dish was filled. I mixed a cup of melted butter with a half cup of sugar and the juice of one lemon, a tablespoon of nutmeg, four whole eggs, and two egg yolks, and poured it over the peaches. Then I put the dish in the oven to bake at 325 degrees F. for about an hour. The juice of the sweet, ripe peaches combined with the eggs and created a velvety-soft custard.

After dinner we finished with a bottle of cold white wine and Mona sweet-talked us into another (competitive) game of Pictionary.

Saturday, August 8

ON OUR FIRST DAY in Savonnieres we had noticed the *La Saponaria*—a masted, square-rigged, wooden boat perhaps forty feet long, with a great wooden rudder and a cabin sitting in the middle of the deck. It was moored in the river just below the campground at the edge of the village. It was this boat that had carried the grain upriver to the mill and back again as milled flour on the day of the Donkey Festival. Jack speculated that the name was derived from the flower saponaria (soapwort or bouncing bet), which grows abundantly in the sandy wastes along the roadsides and is depicted on the signs entering and leaving Savonnieres.

At Madeline and Helmut's engagement ceremony, the priest had explained that the boat was a reproduction of the river barges used in the region before the advent of railroads and trucks. It had been an impressive sight returning under full sail during the Donkey Festival. *La Saponaria*, the priest had informed us, was managed by a local association (les Bateliers du Cher), to which he himself belonged, and was maintained with the proceeds from chartered trips up and down the riverways. The longest of these voyages lasted for several days and followed the Loire all the way out to the Atlantic. Such an expedition was beyond anything we wished to undertake in the time remaining to us, but a day trip along the Cher to the mill and back seemed an altogether romantic proposition, and following some further inquiry, Lettie and Mona arranged for reservations that afternoon, leaving at three.

Just before noon, with Mackie, Agnes, Lettie, and Rory off in Tours, Mona and Jack and I took a walk, climbing a long staircase in the steep hillside behind the church, to a place where the priest had told us a convent had once stood. Tradition has it that saying a rosary on each of these one hundred steps will grant an answer to any prayer. But, perhaps feeling it ungrateful to be asking more in our present happiness (although a little relief from the heat would have been nice), we abjured the rigors of this demanding devotional exercise.

At the top of the climb, we found ourselves on a path that led into a shaded trail through overgrown brush and low-hanging trees that completely obscured any view of the town below. We carefully made our way onward until we encountered a rusted iron gate hanging precariously by one hinge. It was affixed with a small crucifix and opened onto the same heavy growth that had surrounded the trail. As we stepped through to the other side, I had an odd feeling of something hallowed and forbidding about this place. Perhaps Mona felt it as well.

"Maybe we shouldn't be wandering around in here," she said.

We turned and passed back through the gate, touching the crucifix for luck as we left. We followed the trail until it brought us down on the other side of the town, where we circled around and headed back to the main street.

It was just past one when we set ourselves down under an umbrella at the Marina and shared a carafe of red wine while waiting for our lunch to be served. Madame brought out the plat du jour, a pork steak with ratatouille and hunks of fresh baguettes to dip in the pork juice.

"How will we ever return to life in Maine?" Jack joked, savoring a forkful of the meat.

"Well, we can't," Mona replied. "We're going to have to stay here for the rest of our lives."

The silence that followed the statement gave rise to the thought that perhaps it was not a joke.

On the way back to the house I realized that I had neglected to shop, and since the car was in Tours, I stopped at the local boucherie while the others went on without me. Inside, I took my place at the end of a long line. The two butchers were very entertaining. This wasn't simply cutting meat.

This was an art form. Holding the pieces, always carving toward themselves, knowing the precise thickness or trimming off just enough fat to lighten the scales yet leaving enough for flavor, they engaged the customers in animated conversation. I could tell they were a wealth of information concerning the preparation of the meats, and had I been able to understand the language better, I might have avoided what turned out to be the unfortunate results of my uninformed selection.

As I waited my turn I perused the meat counter, trying to decipher the names of the meats and prices scrawled in a gracefully illegible French hand. Even as a chef, I felt out of my element. I first considered a huge *poule noire* (a "black chicken"). But with its head still attached and staring up at me with vacant eyes, its rigid talons protruding menacingly, I quickly decided that we had eaten enough chicken. The woman in front of me purchased a large cut of dark-colored meat with a deep yellow fat around it. I thought it was a steak, but the butcher cut it to a thickness of a small roast.

Great, I thought. What a nice change. I'll do a lovely pot roast in red wine with potatoes and carrots.

When my turn came, I held up seven fingers, pointed to the meat, and said, *"S'il vous plâit, pour sept personnes."* To my surprise, instead of one thick-cut roast, the butcher cut four pieces, each about two inches thick. Well, I thought, somewhat surprised, it's obviously steak.

Back at the house, I placed the meat into a marinade of red

wine with lemon slices, olive oil, fresh herbs, shallots, garlic, and the leftover Pimms Cup and put it into the refrigerator.

≈ ≈ ≈

SOMETIME AFTER TWO O'CLOCK everyone returned from Tours. They had been shopping at les Halles and brought back three kinds of cheese: an inexpensive but tasty blue; an exquisite Camembert; and a small wedge of a slightly sharp, semisoft cheese with a thick brown crust. There were fresh strawberries, zucchini, carrots, tiny little fingerling potatoes, a great hunk of butter, and fresh artichokes. Two of the artichokes were in bloom with colossal purple flowers, which Lettie put into a small vase. I told them of my trip to the boucherie and opened the refrigerator door to show them the marinating steaks.

"You've been doing all of the cooking. Let me *grill* them for you," Mackie suggested. Like most men, he was vain about his prowess with the open flame and anxious for an opportunity to display his "primal" capacities.

"I look forward to any event in which someone is cooking for me," I answered, happily agreeing to his request.

By now it was time to head off for our excursion on the *La Saponaria*.

On boarding, the captain immediately served us each a glass of wine. Beside the five crew members and the seven of us, there was one other passenger, a lady friend of one of the crewmen—thirteen people in all. Since I am always alert to the catastrophic possibilities of any mode of travel, the number was ominous to me and, given the size of the boat, frankly a little too tight. Unfortunately, there was insufficient wind for the sails, so we putted slowly upriver, powered by an inboard motor. The captain continued to ply us with wine the whole way. By the third glass, the boat had begun to feel more cozy than crowded, and I decided the current didn't appear particularly vigorous as I calculated the distance of the swim to shore. Two of the crewmen began to sing, and by the third stanza, we were following—after a fashion. When the song was over we applauded while the captain refilled our glasses. Now, if ever, was the perfect opportunity for us to perform the songs that Lettie had been teaching us in the weeks past. We began with the round *"Hibou et Coucou"* ("The Owl and the Cuckoo") following it with *"Chevaliers de la Table Ronde,"* the drinking song, in which the crew exuberantly joined. Rory, who had been restricted to a single glass of wine, began looking for a lifeboat.

For all of the wine we had drunk since arriving in France, none of us ever felt as though we were getting even tipsy. I don't know if it was the sun, or if we'd simply exceeded our limits this day, but with each glass our singing seemed to get better and better. We sounded fabulous. When Mackie and I launched into a rendition of "Moonlight Bay" in two parts, I was convinced I could not only sing tenor, but that my harmony was enviable. Well, maybe I did get a little blotto . . .

By four o'clock we rounded the last bend and the mill

appeared, as it had stood through so many long summer days before this one. The captain shut down the motor and the crew dropped anchor. We sat for a while moored peacefully. It was wonderful to see this now-familiar terrain from the vantage point of the water. Small birds flitted through the thickets along the bank. The heat and the stillness of the water made us drowsy and content, but soon it was time for our return.

On the way back, the crew unfurled the sails with great flourish and hopefulness, but there was still insufficient wind, and alas, the sails were, once again, furled. It was six o'clock before we finally drifted back to the dock where we had boarded. The crew insisted on opening a last bottle of champagne, and when a beautiful black woman with a baguette under one arm and two teenage girls in tow passed, they waved her aboard to share a drink with us. In the course of our conversation, she explained that her mother was from Savonnieres and had met her father in the Congo. She now spent her summers vacationing here. The two girls, her nieces, were very pretty, and I wondered what Rory thought of them, but secreted behind the mirrors of his sunglasses, he let nothing slip. When we had finished the wine we all shook hands, said our good-byes, and trudged back uphill to the house.

Dinner

Grilled Meat and a Nice Green Salad

THAT EVENING, THE HEAT having lingered from the day, we carried the dining table out onto the terrace for dinner. We were all very hungry and would have eaten earlier except for a problem with the grill. Using some scrap wood from the caves, Mackie started a fire, which unexpectedly flared quickly into high flames. Given the dryness of the long hot spell, I stopped dead in my tracks carrying out the marinated meat, somewhat alarmed. The flames were so bright that they lit up the garden.

"Hey, what's going on?" I heard Mona yell from somewhere in the house just as Lettie, carrying a pot of water, pushed me aside and ran to the grill, and dousing the fire, created a loud sizzle and a mushroom cloud of steam.

"Cool," Rory observed quietly.

"Is everything all right?" Jack called from our bedroom window.

Shaking his head as he stared down into the steaming, soggy ashes, Mackie wore an expression of guilt, fright, surprise, and disappointment. The pride of his grilling acumen evaporated with the steam. But cautiously tipping the grill to spill the excess water, he confidently assured the rest of us,

"This is nothing. I can fix this," and began to rebuild the fire, an effort that was complicated by the bottom of the grill now being filled with wet ashes.

It was another hour before the fire was ready. Ceremoniously, Mackie placed the marinated meat on the grill. With a flourish he added more herbs and turned the pieces over, sprinkling pepper and garlic to the other side as the flames sparked with the hot grease of the meat. It smelled wonderful, like a Lorelei for the nose. When the meat was done, he took it off the grill, cut the pieces in halves, laid them on a platter, and proudly placed it in the center of the table to our expectant applause. Famished, we lifted glasses of Cabernet Sauvignon in a toast to his efforts, hoisted the steaks onto our plates, and began to cut.

And cut we did.

"I think this knife is dull," Jack said.

Finally, we managed to saw off pieces small enough to chew, and sat, masticating like a herd of cows, staring at each other with an expectant glaze in our eyes, as though if we chewed long enough, the meat would become wonderfully sumptuous. Instead it only got tougher.

"What kind of meat did you say this was?" Mackie asked.

"Beefsteaks, I thought," I answered sheepishly, explaining "I couldn't read the signs, but from the way the butcher cut them, I assumed they were steaks."

"I don't think this is beef," Mona opined between chews. "Do you think you might have gotten horse?"

Rory stopped chewing as though digesting the thought of digesting horse. Gingerly he took a swallow of his milk and continued eating.

We were thankful for the large green salad Lettie had prepared. Not only was it delicious, but also, next to the mystery meat, easy on the gums.

Sunday, August 9

I NEVER TIRED OF my morning trip to the patisserie, and with less than a week now before our return home, I tried to imagine myself back in Maine. In South Berwick, a town comparable in size to Savonnieres, we have a gas-station/market and a Dunkin' Donuts. The closest place where I could find anything resembling what was available here each morning was fifteen miles away. It was a thirty-mile drive as opposed to a ten-minute walk before I could sit with coffee and croissant, I realized with some apprehension. I wasn't sure how I was ever going to cope when I got home.

Along with the usual purchases from the patisserie, I served melons I had bought at a farm down the road from Abelard and Simone's house. About the size of a tenpin bowling ball, they had a pale green-gray skin with darker green stripes. The flesh had the color and flavor of cantaloupe but tasted infinitely sweeter. I served the melons cut into wedges and laid them out on a blue-and-white platter in a flower design, with a pink rose at the center.

After breakfast, I braved the heat and took a walk out to the sunflower fields, greeting them as old friends. The river looked so inviting, I sat on the bank, and sheltered from the sun in the shade of a clump of poplars, I watched the lazy flow of the river, just enjoying the tranquillity, which was interrupted only by an occasional magpie. I thought about the renewing affect of the pleasure of sharing friendship and meals together in that beautiful old house in this wonderful countryside. It had reignited my enthusiasm for cooking, and I wondered how it could be preserved once we had returned to our normal lives. The answer to that question, I now saw, had been a major part of the motivation for my undertaking this adventure.

≈ ≈ ≈

BY THE TIME I got back, the temperature had soared to 104 degrees for the second day in a row. Too hot to cook! There were peaches, melons, strawberries, the cheeses that Lettie had bought at les Halles, and an extra baguette from breakfast. We drank an ice-cold Riesling and nibbled on these delicacies under the shade of the boxwood.

Dinner

Parisian Fish Soup with Saffron Rice
Green Salad
Tart Mona

IN SPITE OF THE heat, the house remained quite comfortable. With the draperies pulled and the doors and windows closed, the thick limestone walls kept the interior wonderfully cool.

I had a taste for what I call my Parisian fish soup. This recipe comes from a soup I ate in Paris fifteen years ago and is so delicious it has become part of my regular repertoire. I began by frying a pound of bacon, cut into tiny pieces, until it was crisp. Then I drained off the grease and added a small can of tomato extract and four small chopped green onions. I turned the flame down to medium, stirring continuously as the tomato paste browned.

As I said before, when you use tomato paste as a base, the darker brown you can sauté it without burning, the better your sauce or soup will taste. When it was a rich, russet color, I added two large cans of plum tomatoes with their juices, four cups of fish stock (made from bouillon), half a bottle of a good dry red wine, four medium-size carrots sliced thinly, about two cups of chopped and washed leeks from the garden, a cup of chopped fennel, and two large diced red peppers.

Bringing it to a boil, I added some salt, pepper, and fresh tarragon, then turned it down and let it simmer for just about two hours.

By this time the broth had thickened, and I added a mixture of approximately two pounds of fish—a boned red snapper and three kinds of filleted whitefish whose name I didn't know since I couldn't make out the words in French and no one at the market could tell me what they were in English. They were great-looking fish—that's all that mattered to me. I let the kettle simmer for another half hour until the fish began to fall apart.

While the soup was cooking I boiled up some rice, seasoned it with saffron, and served it with the hot, tomato, winy *"potage de poissons à la Parisienne"* ladled over it. Bread with butter and a small green salad were the accompaniments.

≈ ≈ ≈

I HAD PICKED UP a large container of Nutella after Mona had brought back a tiny jar of it from the market a few days earlier.

"This is the greatest stuff in the world!" she raved, eating it with a spoon right out of the jar.

"It's like chocolate peanut butter," Jack marveled, tasting a spoonful for himself.

I wasn't entirely certain how I wanted to make this Nutella dessert, but I began by laying a puff-pastry round into the buttered tart dish. I pulled out the blender and began by adding five whole eggs with three extra yolks, two cups of Nutella, two cups of crème fraîche, and four tablespoons of flour. As an afterthought I added a tablespoon of cinnamon. When it had blended, I poured it into the puff pastry and baked it at 300 degrees F. until it set up—about forty-five minutes. When it was done, I put it into the freezer briefly to cool it off before moving it to the refrigerator. Just before serving, I spread the top with crème fraîche. I called it Tarte Mona. The consistency of the tart was a little like a cheese-cake. Everyone liked it, but I would have preferred it to be smoother, more like a custard, and I determined that the next time I would leave the flour and crème fraîche out of the mixture entirely and just use the crème fraîche as a topping.

Monday, August 10

THIS WAS AGNES'S BIRTHDAY, and after breakfast I drove the sisters into Balin-Mire, where Lettie had seen "just the cake" she wanted for the party. Unfortunately we arrived to discover that the patisserie was closed on Mondays.

"I knew I should have picked it up yesterday," Lettie repeated obsessively.

"They have wonderful cakes in Savonnieres," Mona offered soothingly. "Let's see if they're open."

With a sense of urgency, I sped the car back across the hills into Savonnieres. The town was busy for a Monday morning, with a line out on the sidewalk in front of the patisserie. Dropping the sisters off in front, I told them to meet me in the little lot next to the river, and before long, they appeared carrying two boxes nicely wrapped and tied.

"They were so beautiful we got a couple of things," Lettie said, delighted now. "I couldn't resist—you'll see when we get back to the house."

Agnes was in the shower when we returned, preparing for an excursion into Tours, where her mother and aunt wanted to treat her to some birthday shopping. We quickly opened the boxes to examine the desserts. In the first there was a cake with a bottom and top layer of génoise (French sponge cake) filled with a thick strawberry mousse. The top was covered in a clear strawberry gelatin with a lovely decoration of fleur-de-lis piped on in chocolate. The second box held a tart—a butter pastry filled with fresh raspberries, also coated with a gelatin, so that the fruit seemed suspended under glass, like an elegant paperweight.

Later that morning Rory, Mackie, and the three women piled into the car and headed out for Tours. Rory had decided to give the cyber café a second chance and Mackie had been elected to be the driver.

While Jack retired upstairs to read, I took a long walk into the hills up past Simone and Abelard's, circling back around to the other side of the village. Returning to the house, I suggested a late lunch and Jack and I walked back into town to the Marina. It was so pleasant in the little garden behind the café—cool, despite the heat, under the shade of the hillside that rose up sharply behind—that we lingered for some time there. It was three o'clock before we got back, and still the others hadn't returned. Delighted by this opportunity to cook without interruption, I busied myself with preparations for the evening's celebration.

Agnes's Birthday Dinner

Baked Snails in Butter, Lemon, and Parsley
Breast of Duck in a Crème de Cassis Sauce
Chartreuse of Vegetables
Strawberry Mousse Génoise and Raspberry Tart

WE HAD DECIDED ON a menu of duck breast in a crème de cassis sauce served with a chartreuse of vegetables and an appetizer of snails in a lemon, garlic, and parsley butter.

To begin the chartreuse, I peeled about five pounds of red potatoes, which I boiled in lightly salted water. While the potatoes were cooking, I julienned and parboiled five or six medium-size carrots along with thin slices of summer squash and zucchinis (two of each), a half-dozen brussels sprouts, a couple of fleurettes of cauliflower, six cabbage leaves, and about a pound and a half of string beans. Since I hadn't found fresh peas, I substituted a bag of frozen. It's important that all the vegetables (with the exception of the peas) be slightly cooked and cooled before the construction begins.

When the potatoes had boiled long enough, I drained them, added a cup of crème fraîche, four tablespoons of chopped roasted garlic, a quarter cup of butter, salt, and pepper, and mashed them until they were smooth. Then I set them aside to cool.

When this was done, I took a soufflé dish, slathering the bottom and sides with enough butter (at least a quarter of a pound) to hold the cooled vegetables when pressed into it. Next I laid a ring of peas around the bottom of the dish, followed by a ring of overlapping zucchini slices, then an overlapping ring of summer squash, alternating in this fashion until the bottom of the dish was covered. Around the sides I alternated the julienne carrot sticks with the string beans.

Next, adding the mashed potatoes, I carefully covered the bottom so as not to disturb the design, pushing more up against the sides like a plaster to hold the carrots and string beans in place. The potatoes should be at least two inches thick, creating a well in the center to be lined neatly with two of the cabbage leaves, pressed firmly into the potatoes. Into this well I laid a ring of brussels sprouts with the cauliflower at the center, then covered it over with another cabbage leaf, covered that with more potatoes, and another double ring of squash and zucchini, finally covering it all with the remaining potatoes. I used a pair of scissors to trim off any of the carrots and string beans sticking up over the top of the dish.

By five-thirty the others had returned from Tours, and while they where dressing for dinner I began preparing the duck.

In a small saucepan I put three cups of crème de cassis, two large shallots chopped, a half cup of a strong Dijon mustard, and the juice and zest of one orange. I brought the mixture to a light simmer, eventually reducing it by half—which left a thick, deep purple syrup. Setting this to the side, I placed the four duck breasts onto a cooking rack over a sheet pan and put them into a 350 degree F. oven to cook slowly, reducing the shrinkage and leaving them just slightly on the pink side. This took about half an hour. I removed the duck, turned the heat up to 425 degrees and placed the chartreuse in the oven for twenty minutes.

I prepared the snails with a simple filling of butter, lemon, parsley, garlic, salt, and pepper and placed them on a small baking sheet ready for the broiler.

I cut each duck breast into thin slices and laid them into a terra-cotta baking dish. I poured off the fat from the baking pan, added the duck juices to the cassis mixture, letting it simmer for a few more minutes, then poured it over the duck and placed the baking dish back in the oven for a few minutes.

Meantime, Mackie and Rory lit the candles and set the table, which Lettie and Mona had decorated with a dozen bright little bouquets from the garden, using the crème caramel jars that Mona had salvaged for vases. We all donned our wreaths and shouted "Surprise!" when Agnes appeared. Her mother placed a crown of green leaves and yellow flowers on her head and took her in her arms, not unlike the way she had so many times before. Agnes looked lovely, flushed with surprise, her beautiful blond hair freshly brushed and hanging loose about her shoulders, a broad, slightly embarrassed smile crossing her face. We lifted glasses of champagne in her honor, and as everyone took their places in anticipation of the banquet, I brought on the first course of snails. When we had finished them, Jack and Mackie cleared away the dishes while I removed the chartreuse from the oven, covered it with a platter, inverted it, and carefully lifted the soufflé dish. The result was a beautiful piece of freestanding edible sculpture. As everyone applauded this success, I proudly set the duck before Agnes. I felt that I had reached a summit with this meal, one of the few times in thirty years of cooking that I felt completely gratified with my own creation.

The sauce was one of the best of my career. A perfect blend of ingredients that was an exquisite complement to the slightly rare duck breast. Mona was moved to tears. The chartreuse was faultless, the orange, yellow, and green of the vegetables a colorful tribute to the monks who first invented it, perfectly accented by the green and yellow of the crowns and the bright little bouquets scattered informally across the table.

Seated around the candlelit table, the festive crowns of flowers and leaves gracing our heads like a company of Olympians, we toasted Agnes, lit the candles on the cake, and sang a joyous "Happy Birthday." We devoured the cake and the tart afterward like a pack of ravenous wolves.

LETTIE WANTED AGNES TO see the beautiful château of Azay-le-Rideau, which she had visited on her honeymoon, and invited Jack and me to accompany them there. Azay-le-Rideau is not far from Savonnieres, and leaving the house by eleven-thirty that morning, we arrived in time for an early lunch at the Hôtel Balzac on the outskirts of town. Once again, the food at this randomly chosen place was excellent, with a comfortable dining room that looked out onto a prim little garden of geraniums, clipped boxwood, and gravel. Agnes ordered a salad, while the rest of us had full meals. I chose the lamb and both Lettie and Jack ordered the veal, each served with a nice little salad in a simple oil-and-vinegar dressing, roasted potatoes, green beans, some delicious bread, and a carafe each of a local red and white wine. The lamb was very good, but the veal was exceptional, served in a brown sauce made with white wine and shallots and seasoned with just a hint of thyme. For dessert, a delectable apricot tart was served with coffee.

Unlike the other châteaux we visited, with their symmetrical designs of long avenues and clipped parterres, Azay is in the English style, surrounded by an extensive park that, after two centuries, has come into an impressive maturity. At home, the symmetrical style is seldom undertaken, and to see it accomplished with such stunning effect in France, its place of origin, in all of its precision and clarity, had been a treat. But the park and garden here at Azay reminded me of the aesthetic pleasures of our own, more informal English-derived mode.

The superb trees—wonderful specimens of ginkgo, cypress, and cedar, along with indigenous varieties—were a great refreshment on this very hot afternoon. We followed the gravel paths that move among them through numerous, tree-framed views of this glorious palace, its image inverted in the surrounding lake that had been enlarged from the moat of a medieval fortification that once stood on this site.

Inside, a galleried staircase of three flights divides the château down the center, so as you make your way from one end of each floor to the other, you repeatedly pass through this beautifully proportioned, dignified space, cooled by the ventilation of the double windows that open on each landing.

Such magnificence creates an illusion of stability, immovable as the great stones of the foundation on which the whole improbable edifice is resting. The remorseless necessities of daily life would seem to have been banished here. But reviewing the historical sketch of its occupants (supplied in the brochure we'd received when purchasing our tickets) reminded me that you could find yourself as precariously perched in a château as in a hovel, that possessions and wealth, which free us from want, also incite rapacity and greed.

The builder of the château, a finance minister to the king and lord to a handsomely endowed dame, had fallen under suspicion of corruption and beat an abrupt retreat into a distant country. Leaving his affluent wife and possessions in the dust, he escaped imprisonment and execution. The château had weathered the revolution, but impoverished after the collapse of the Second Empire, the descendants of those who had laid out the wonderful park had sold it piecemeal. You can't live in a palace and cut corners!

The kitchens alone must have taken a dozen people to manage, between the cooks and bakers and scullery. I stopped to admire an enormous quantity of copperware and fantasized about cooking in the huge, open fireplace. But even in my daydreams, the work of feeding a castleful of people seemed staggering. Apart from the gentry and their constant houseguests, there were the master's personal maids, servants for everyone else, groundskeepers, and gamekeepers, not to mention the stable crowd. I'm thinking maybe Cinderella didn't get such a great deal after all.

~ ~ ~

ON THE WAY BACK TO the car we passed a small grocery with a box in the window filled with what looked to be enormous pink grapes. Taken by their color and size, I went in to examine them and discovered that they were mirabelles—not large grapes at all but ripe little plums. The grocer offered me one. It was so sweet and delicious that I purchased a bagful, which we ate on the ride home, saving a mere handful for our compatriots at the house.

When we got back to Savonnieres, a traffic cop stopped us by the bridge for a long line of cars that was crossing the river out of the village. Waiting there in the intense heat, we became parched, and when Agnes raced into a café for a bottle of cold water, the bartender explained that there had been a funeral.

At long last we were allowed to proceed. Back at the house, Mackie told us he had run into the priest that morning who had given him the news. "Ahh, a tragedy," he had said. "A young man . . . only twenty-six." And then he mimed injecting a needle into his arm. The pitiful story seemed completely incongruous in this place.

But we really didn't live here. We couldn't read the papers or understand the news on TV. We didn't have to find a job and a place to live. We really didn't know what life for the average person was as we sat in our walled garden, away from the stark, unhappy realities that can sometimes pull people apart. It seemed unfair to make a judgment. Despair has no boundaries. It just seemed more sorrowful given the happiness we had known in this place for the past month.

❧

Dinner

Leftover Mystery Meat Soup

FOR DINNER I MADE a soup by combining the trimmings left from the vegetable chartreuse, with the remains of the mystery meat, a few cut-up carrots and onions, a half bottle of a cheap white wine with six cups of beef stock, and some fresh, chopped tomatoes, all of which I let simmer for about an hour.

There was about a cup of mashed potatoes left from the chartreuse that I mixed with one egg yolk and a couple of tablespoons of flour until it became just thick enough to roll into long strips. I cut the strips into one-inch pieces like gnocci, gave them a slight twist and added them to the soup about five minutes before serving.

It was a great meal, despite the mystery meat, which, mysteriously, seemed tougher. I had begun to think it might be rhino, or perhaps hippo. (It wasn't until I had been home for several months and described the meat to a chef from France that I learned we had been eating wild boar and that the meat should have been braised . . . *never* grilled.)

Wednesday, August 12

AGNES WAS LEAVING ON an early train out of Tours that morning, and Lettie, who was seeing her off at the station, offered to pick up the tickets for our own departure on Saturday. Remembering Madeline and Helmut's leave-taking, I suggested that we go first class.

"This has been too wonderful a time to end up pushing and shoving to get in a crowded car," I said.

"He's right!" Mackie agreed without hesitation. "Get first class."

As it turned out, because we were traveling as a group and with a minor, there was an enormous discount. Had I thought to remind Lettie that I was over sixty, we could have paid still less. Even so, subtracting the discounts, we paid only a few dollars more than for second class.

That afternoon, Jack and I took our last walk out to the mill at Balin, arriving once again at the nearby café just minutes after two o'clock.

"*Fermé!*" the proprietor insisted without apology when I inquired about the plat du jour. Once again we ordered Badouit and "*sandwich jambon avec fromage*" (ham with, for a change, cheese). At a table nearby, a party sat laughing and joking, enjoying what looked like lovely food. I was more convinced than ever that the owner hated Americans. A little while afterward, his wife, who was apparently the cook, appeared with a tray full of beefsteak dinners served with french fries. The party, a crowd in their fifties and sixties who'd been drinking and were sharing a nice pâté, greeted her exuberantly. Setting a plate in front of each, she wished them *bon appetit* and disappeared without acknowledging us. Now I was convinced that not only the proprietor but his wife as well hated Americans.

Still, it was pleasant sitting under the pavilion out of the heat. The other party was very entertaining. Not that we were eavesdropping; it was more like a French lesson. Recognizing an occasional word or phrase, we amused ourselves with wild guesses at what they might be saying.

When it was time to pay the bill, I went inside. The owner muttered the amount.

"I don't understand," I answered in my flawed French.

The owner wrote the amount on a slip of paper. Studying it carefully, I felt pretty sure that it said sixty-five francs, so I laid out that amount, repeating it in French, as a question rather than as a statement. The mood suddenly reversing itself, the man repeated the amount, smiling. Once again I repeated the amount. Attempting to correct my pronunciation, he again said, "*Soixante-cinq.*"

This time I managed to reproduce the accent perfectly, and, pleased by my effort, both of us smiled.

"*Merci monsieur. Bon voyage,*" he said.

"You know what?" I began as we headed back down the road to the river. "He doesn't hate Americans. I'll bet he thought we were English."

"Why do you say that?" Jack asked.

"Well, you know the French have never been crazy for the English."

More generous than I, Jack suggested, "Maybe he's just tired of tourists. Remember how you felt about tourists when you had the restaurant?" Although I appreciated the benevolence of this reasoning, I was still certain we had been mistaken for British.

≈ ≈ ≈

BEFORE ANY OF US left the house that morning, the fuel men had arrived to fill the oil tank for the hot water heater and Marie-Claire appeared with the key to the utility room. When the men had finished, they returned the keys, and Marie-Claire, who was chatting with Mona and Lettie, absentmindedly set them on the table beside the set of house keys that Lettie had taken down in preparation for her departure to Tours. By this time Jack and I had already gone, taking the second set of house keys with us. When Marie-Claire left at the same time as everyone else, she offered to lock the gate after them as they drove away.

When the group returned later that afternoon, they were mystified to discover that none of the keys would fit the gate. After much discussion it was finally decided that they must have picked up the wrong set of keys and were locked out. Remembering a ladder stored in one of the caves, Mackie hoisted Rory up over the wall and into the garden. Hearing the commotion, the lady across the street came to her window, and when Lettie explained the situation, she graciously supplied some chairs for the comfort of the sisters as they waited.

By the time Rory returned and lowered the ladder down to his father, all of our elderly neighbors up and down Rue de la Liberté had appeared at their windows and doors to discuss the proceedings. Even Monsieur Deek barked an opinion from his accustomed perch. Shaking their heads, they watched the "Américains" climbing over the wall, laughing and saying things we weren't certain we wanted translated.

⟋⟍

Dinner

Cold Sorrel Vichyssoise
Rhubarb—Plum—Crème de Cassis Sauce on Vanilla Ice Cream

WE DIDN'T WANT TO leave a lot of food behind in the refrigerator, and with so little time remaining, decided to make do with what was left from our last trip to the ATAC. There were a few potatoes, a couple leeks, and some sorrel left in the garden, so I made a sorrel vichyssoise.

First I diced the potatoes, sautéing them with the leeks in butter until they were soft. I then added about a cup of leftover Riesling from the refrigerator, letting it simmer for another ten minutes, before adding a quart and a half of fresh whole milk and about four cups of the chopped sorrel. Stirring continuously, I brought it to a boil, seasoned it with salt and pepper, turned it off, and poured it into a large baking dish that I put into the freezer to chill.

Meanwhile, Mona had gathered a bunch of rhubarb from the garden. "You know," she suggested, "it would really be nice to do something with this. We haven't used it once since we've been here."

I diced it (about three cups), put it into a saucepan with a cup of sugar, a cup of plum jam, and a cup of crème de cassis, letting it simmer into a dark red sauce, sweet but just tart enough to make your mouth pucker. I set it aside to let it cool.

When the soup was cold, I whipped it smooth in the blender and served it with baguettes and butter. For dessert we had the rhubarb-plum-cassis sauce over vanilla ice cream.

Later that evening we were pleasantly surprised by a phone call from Madeline. It had taken her and Helmut all this time to feel that they had somewhat readjusted to life stateside. "The first week back," she grumbled, "was dreadful." She hated everything—the bread, the butter, even the coffee. The flight back had been as lamentable as the flight over, and on their first morning Helmut had announced that he "wasn't getting out of bed until *Buddy* had made the coffee and gone down for baguettes." I felt it was a great tribute.

Thursday, August 13

ON THE EVENING OF our return from Paris, Mackie had talked with great enthusiasm about having visited Amboise and in particular the château le Clos-Luce, the house where Leonardo da Vinci had spent the last three years of his life. To leave France without seeing this extraordinary residence would have been a great mistake, and over breakfast, Jack and I decided that it was a trip we would make that morning. With the coffee cups and dishes cleared away, we got into the car, waved good-bye, and headed out.

At last the long hot spell had broken. The sky was again a cloudlessly cool and dark blue. North of Tours, the road began following the Loire through a countryside less populated than that surrounding Savonnieres. With only an occasional farmhouse, the land appeared drier and flatter. People fished and camped at the edge of the broad river or waded in the cool water that never seemed more than waist deep.

It was still early when we arrived at Amboise, parked the car, and headed up the long, narrow street to the top of the hill and the château le Clos-Luce.

François I had bestowed the house on da Vinci with a yearly stipend of seven hundred golden crowns. He arrived in 1515 with Francesco de Melzi, his prótegé (and companion), many years his junior; one servant, Battista de Villanis; and three paintings wrapped in leather bags and tied to a mule: *St. John the Baptist, Virgin and Child with St. Anne,* and, incredibly, the *Mona Lisa.* The thought of him traveling from Italy to France carrying the *Mona Lisa* tied to a mule is stunning.

The house was not yet crowded with visitors, and we were able to walk comfortably from room to room. Standing before the bed where the great genius had died, touching the door handles he had once touched, feeling the stone of the fireplace of his room, we were humbled and inspired.

From the windows of his study we could view the great castle of his benefactor, François I, not far from where we stood. The château Amboise, once the domain of splendor, also had a darker, more sinister history.

In 1560, Protestants plotted to force religious concessions from François II, the son of François I and Catherine de Medici. Upon learning of it, he had twelve hundred of the conspirators slaughtered. As a warning to anyone who might want to reincite rebellion, he had the bodies hung from the castle and walls of the town, even suspending cadavers from trees throughout the city. The event was so horrifying that the reputation and power of the great castle created by his parents began slowly to erode and over the years disappeared completely. In the course of time, parts of the castle had even been dismantled.

It was a bizarre irony, standing in this room of so much vision and creativity, viewing the place that held such a fearful legend. I was eager to turn my back on this dreaded memorial in favor of the airiness that filled the halls that held the memory of Leonardo da Vinci. We strolled through the house, admiring the rooms, examining the frescos painted by Leonardo's students in the small chapel, passing through the dining hall, until at last we arrived at the kitchen.

We rested there for a long time. I studied the fireplace with its iron rings once used to hang game that were spit-roasted and basted with hot wine. The bread bin, copper dishes, stone sink, and the long, rough-hewn table all filled my imagination with thoughts of the food that must have been cooked there.

The *Mona Lisa* in Italian is called *La Giaconda*. There is cake, attributed to the French, made of ground almonds, sugar, and egg yolks folded into a meringue and called a *jaconde*. It was named after the painting. I wondered if per-

haps this was the very kitchen where it had been first con-
cocted for the delight of the master.

Throughout the rooms were framed quotations of da
Vinci. On a staircase leading to his workroom in the lower
part of the house I came across one entitled *On Work*. The
translation read: *Oh God, you sell all things to men at the
cost of their effort.*

For as long as I could remember, the fear that I would
never succeed in my struggles, that I would never be good
enough, had gripped me. But here, in this house of light, were
the words from a man whose faith assured me that it was
simply the *effort* that made me good enough. I felt, at long
last, at the age of sixty-one, released from that distant limbo
of my childhood.

We left the house, passing through the small Italianate
garden at the rear and then followed the path to the park that
surrounded the house. Centuries-old trees lined the walks
and shaded the grass, where people sat eating sandwiches. A
group of small children, led by a teenage girl, played a ring
game in a clearing by the stream.

≈ ≈ ≈

BACK IN SAVONNIERES THAT afternoon, we accompanied Lettie
to the Marina Café for one last lunch—beefsteak with french
fries served with a pâté and salad, a carafe of red wine, and
for dessert, a prune-and-raisin torte. Lettie complimented

Madame on the cake, as we did on the entire lunch, and she offered to give her the recipe. I was surprised to see her bring a page from a magazine. I just assumed everyone in France was simply a wonderful cook by instinct. I couldn't imagine anyone using a recipe. Creating one certainly, but using one? Hmmph! *Je suis très amazed!* But, I found it to be such an interesting cake I thought it should be shared.

FARCI BRETON

200 grams powdered sugar

4 eggs

3/4 liter milk

250 grams flour

spoonful of rum (the amount is up to the baker)

50 grams raisins

12 pitted prunes

Whip together the sugar, eggs, milk, flour, and rum, add the prunes and raisins, put the mixture into a buttered cake pan, and bake at 325 degrees F. for about an hour.

After lunch I set off on a final walk out to the sunflowers, stopping once again to admire the stone farmhouse that sits by the river where the road turns abruptly back into the yellow fields behind. The wonderful blue-green front door that faces out toward the river stands above stone steps covered in masses of deep green moss. A magenta hydrangea was blooming against the light gray of the limestone wall. The combination of the color and form was all so beautiful that I determined I must return and photograph it.

As I turned the corner, my attention was caught by a massive shrub of lavender that grew in a little bit of yard behind the house. Then I looked up in anticipation of the great yellow sunflowers and was completely taken aback. The entire field had turned gray. The heads drooped as though in a great sadness, which I imagined was for me, because I was leaving. Thanking them for this gesture of commiseration, I bade them an affectionate *au revoir*, touched by their show of friendship at my impending departure.

Dinner

Cream of Leek Soup
Salad
Crème Caramel

IN THE REFRIGERATOR THERE were still a dozen or so petits suisses, a couple of crème and café caramels in their little glass jars, several hunks of unfinished cheese, almost all of the "goat honey," a few chocolate bars, some white wine and champagne, and a handful of carrots, tomatoes, and string beans.

I gathered up the last of the leeks from the garden. In a soup pot I melted a cup of butter and stirred in about a cup of flour and a half cup of dry chicken bouillon. When the flour, butter, and bouillon were thoroughly mixed, I added half a bottle of white wine and let the soup simmer until the alcohol had cooked off, then I added a quart of milk. As the mixture thickened on the heat, I added the washed and chopped leeks, seasoned the mix with black pepper and salt, and let it simmer on a low flame until it developed into a creamy leek soup. With it I served the cheese, leftover bread, and a salad of carrots, tomatoes, lettuce, and string beans. We had the crème caramels for dessert.

Friday, August 14

THIS WAS TO BE our last full day at the house, and my walk to the patisserie seemed very important this morning. I looked around at the town as if to fix in my mind forever the bike shop, the markets, the bakeries, the tables overlooking the river where we had enjoyed so many pleasant meals together. I felt as though I had lived here a long time. Long enough for people to recognize me, to smile and wish me *bonjour* when we met. Long enough to feel comfortable and safe here. The house and the town seemed to have become our own.

Tomorrow there wouldn't be time enough for our usual leisurely breakfast; we would be leaving too early for the station. I tried not to dwell on our impending departure as I made the coffee and heated the water for tea, setting the table with the beautiful blue-and-white china and the small coffee mugs with the convenient little lip on the ear for your thumb.

After breakfast, Jack and I decided to make a final trip into Tours. There had been a fine press edition offered by the museum, as a souvenir of the Delacroix exhibition we had attended, of the small bound sketchbook the artist had kept of the Touraine. At the time the price had seemed exorbitant, but since then Jack had regretted his decision to forgo the purchase and I suggested this would be the last opportunity for him to obtain the book. Learning of our plans, Lettie decided to make one last foray into the lace-and-drapery shops and joined us.

We parked the car near a favorite corner café and, agreeing to meet there in a couple of hours for lunch, left on our separate ways.

~ ~ ~

THE YOUNG LADY AT the front desk of the museum shook her head and with a delicate gesture of regret indicated that none of the Delacroix sketchbooks were left. In her somewhat faltering English, she explained that a new order was expected by the end of the week. When I told her that we were leaving in the morning, she invited us to take a seat, and excusing herself for a moment began dialing her phone. There followed a rapid exchange, repeated in a second phone call, after which she smiled in our direction.

"*Voilà*," she said, inviting us back to the desk. There was a store nearby, she explained, with the book in stock.

Taking a pocket-size street map from a drawer, she marked an *X* on the museum and traced a line along the streets we were to follow, marking our destination with another *X* and printing the name of the store at one corner of the map. We were very taken by her thoughtfulness and, following her directions, were able to find the bookstore without any difficulty.

By this time it was nearing noon, and on our way to the café where we had agreed to meet Lettie, we passed what at first appeared to be a patisserie. The window was filled with the most beautiful confections I had ever seen. I couldn't help but stop to admire the display, remarkable pastries that were really small pieces of edible art. Tiny fruit tarts filled with strawberries and peach slices, kiwi and bananas, raspberries and mirabelles; little meringue swans; puff pastry filled with crèmes and custards of different flavors; miniature cakes decorated more elaborately than any wedding cake; chocolate-covered creams and nuts and divinely ornate truffles.

Inside, the showcases displayed a luncheon buffet. There were tapas, little Spanish meat pies folded in half, about the size of a silver dollar. There were two beautifully conceived terrines—one spinach, a long green loaf, filled with orange pieces of carrots; the other fish, alabaster white, artfully infused with a combination of tomatoes, carrots, and mushrooms. There were thinly sliced baked eggplant wrapped around little sausages and a tart of a butter pastry filled with sun-dried tomatoes.

A hostess invited me to be seated, but I replied that I was

simply admiring the magnificent turnout. When I explained that I was a chef, she invited me to see the rest of the buffet on the upper level. There I found more of the same and a masterful display of breads.

"Look," I said, after Jack and I had found Lettie, who was just about to order a cool drink, "I've found this incredible place. We must eat there." Both Jack and Lettie were concerned about the price.

"I'll treat," I insisted, refusing to except a no. "We have to eat there!"

Lettie gathered up her bags and we headed back to the restaurant.

Seeming pleased, the hostess welcomed me back, led us up the stairs to a table on the mezzanine, and handed us each a menu.

Poirault

—

TOURS

Semaine

des

Gourmets

Plats à Emporter

et

Servis au Buffet

Patissier-Chocolatier-Traiteur

———

Inside it listed:

BUFFET D'ENTRÉES

Salade de concombre

Tartare de légumes aux fines herbes

Tarte au basilic, tomates et poivrons

Tapas d'aubergine a l'andalouse

Terrine de la mer à la coriandre

Salade piemontaise

A waitress appeared with carafes of red and white wine. Wearing just a touch of makeup, dressed in a white blouse and blue midlength skirt with slits in the side, she had a naturalness about her that put us entirely at ease. Throughout the meal that followed, her service never had that strained effort to be elegant that comes across as contrived and ends up making the diner feel uncomfortable. This was a woman who had the gift of making you feel gladly received.

I helped myself to the empanada, filled little pastries in a sweet-sour sauce, some of the spicy veal sausages wrapped in eggplant, a slice of the sun-dried tomato tart, and a thin slice each of the spinach and whitefish terrines. Shamelessly I was about to go for a second helping when the waitress arrived with a tray filled with three dishes of steaming food.

"What's this, Lettie?" I asked.

After a short exchange with the waitress, Lettie explained, "*Panache de la mer—petits légumes frais*. With the buffet you also get the entrée, and I think because today is Friday, it's fish."

There were three kinds of fish in a light cream sauce: a smoked whitefish, a perch, and the third, which looked and tasted like sole. The sauce was excellent. On one side of the plate was creamed cauliflower, and on the other side was cauliflower not creamed, which seemed odd, but I liked the idea a lot. This chef really knew his business. His taste was flawless! Wanting him to know how much he had been appreciated, I sent the menu down with the waitress and asked her if she would have the chef autograph it.

As we were eating our desserts of chocolate mousse, fresh strawberries, and an apricot tart, the waitress suggested some ice cream, which was a specialty of the place. Who could say no? We ordered a passion fruit ice cream, a chocolate, and one raspberry.

Blissfully satiated, we finished off the meal with a café grand and lingered for a while before heading downstairs to pay the bill. At the register I thanked the hostess and asked if I might meet the chef. *"Un moment, s'il vous plait,"* she replied, and sent a young woman into the kitchen, who returned moments later with this short, thin kid. He looked like a teenager! We shook hands and I complimented him on his food. One of the waitresses spoke a little English and translated for us. I told him I was a chef from the USA and that I wrote about food and had been knocked out by his artistry and his taste. Thanking me profusely, he spoke and the waitress translated his words as follows:

"My name is Cyril Payraudeau. I am twenty-four years old. I wish to cook in America. I am not married and I have no children."

We shook hands and I promised to keep my ears open.

Twenty-four years old! And he was already a master at what he was doing and working in one of the best places in Tours. How old was he when he realized this talent? Who was it that had discovered it? His parents? Teachers? When did he begin his training? I wondered, with some envy in my admiration, what my own life would have been like had I been able to study cooking as early as this young man obviously had.

~ ~ ~

THAT AFTERNOON I DECIDED that if I was ever going to get a photograph of the farmhouse with the beautiful blue-green door that we passed on our walks to the mill, this was the time. I drove, parking the little car along the road in view of the house, hoping not to disturb the residents. I had already taken several shots, down on one knee photographing the front door and trying to not look like Margaret Bourke-White, when I was startled by an elderly gentleman who had come outside to watch me. He was not smiling.

"*Bonjour monsieur. Votre maison est très jolie!*" I offered awkwardly. ("Good day, sir. Your house is beautiful.")

"*Merci,*" he replied.

We spoke a bit, neither of us understanding too much of what the other was saying, but he invited me around to see the back of the house.

Uh-oh, I thought, following after him. "Is this where I get locked in the barn and he calls the gendarmes?"

Around back, the house and barn formed an L. Overgrown with lavender and wildflowers, the yard within was strewn with hay. Sunlight poured through the open stable doors, illuminating a weathered hay wagon. A stone staircase led up one side to a door on the upper floor at the back of the house. It was the consummate French scene. With the farmer's encouragement I took several pictures.

Miming our conversation as we spoke, we were able to manage some understanding of what the other was saying, and I asked him to stand for a picture. At first he declined, but after some encouragement, he consented. Standing straight and looking very serious, he removed his hat and I snapped a few shots. Not wishing to impose any further, I thanked him and was about to leave, but he insisted I come inside.

He brought me into the kitchen through a narrow back hall, and offering me a seat, disappeared into a pantry. Returning moments later with two glasses and a bottle of homemade wine, he filled the glasses and we toasted each other's health and drank.

When I asked the age of the house, the old man wrote *11 siècle* on a scrap of paper.

"Eleventh century!" It was obvious I was impressed.

Resorting to his paper and pencil again, he was able to convey that the house's foundation had been laid in the eleventh century. The wall of the kitchen, he told me, had been built in the 1300s. It was now covered with school pictures of grandchildren—the girls in pigtails and glasses, the boys in striped shirts with gap-toothed grins.

Smiling in welcome, his wife appeared and joined our conversation. When I asked her if she still used the oven at the back of the fireplace, she replied that she made bread in it all the time, and as her husband was refilling my glass, she proudly directed my attention to a chestnut hutch that had belonged to her grand-mère. Tall and bowed, with brass pulls, it was filled with dishes: pieces of blue-and-white china; pink dinner plates with a floral design; cups and saucers; crystal candlesticks; and saltcellars. Mixed in with this fragile display was her everyday kitchenware: heavy iron skillets and worn copper pots and pans with brass hardware.

When, in the course of my visit, I explained to them where I was from, they seemed genuinely interested to hear about Maine. I was touched by this and by their generosity to me, and as I was attempting to convey what a memorable and grand time this month had been for me, my voice caught and I could feel my face growing flushed. Regaining composure, I finished the wine, and thanking them, requested a last photograph, which I took outside before the beautiful blue-green door—a gentleman with his hat in his hand, a smiling lady, and their little brown-and-white dog. The photograph taken, we made our farewells, and impulsively, I took his wife's hand and lifted it to my lips with a feeling that it was France I was kissing good-bye.

As I drove away, I could see them in my rearview mirror, returning with their little dog to the house. I tooted a last farewell as I rounded the bend. Their friendly acceptance of me had seemed to symbolize the entire success of this trip.

I remembered the birthday at which this adventure had begun and the wish I had made when blowing out the candles. Mona's challenge to our daydream of a house in Europe—*Why don't we do that?*—now seemed almost to have been an answer to that wish, since the dare had really been the seed that had yielded this serendipitous harvest. I had arrived at an impasse, feeling uninspired after thirty years of cooking, thinking a much-needed break would revitalize my interests, but had found instead that it was through the food and cooking every day that not only my interests but my spirit had been renewed.

~ ~ ~

THERE WAS NOTHING LEFT in the house except a couple of chocolate bars, a bottle or two of wine, and some petits suisses, so we agreed to dine out, deciding to give the inn down the street another shot.

It was already late when we arrived. The owner's wife stood staring from the doorway as we approached. Halting before her less-than-warm gaze, we inquired if it was too late for dinner. It was not, she answered, and directing us to follow, brought us out back to the garden, seating us at the same table as we had eaten at before. The food, which had been adequate then, was not really very good this evening. Apparently we had arrived at the end of an extremely busy night. There was an air of frustration and distracted haste in the waitress's service and she made many mistakes. But now, on the eve of our departure, we shared a feeling of contented achievement that even this incommodious dinner was unable to dissipate. On a sudden inspiration I rose, proposing, "A toast. I'd like to make a toast!"

Everyone quieted.

"To the most perfect vacation of my life," I toasted, "and to the house that kept us so comfortable, the garden, the sunflowers, the food, this town . . . and most of all, here's to all of us for making it happen."

We had just lifted our glasses when a young family was seated at the table next to ours. Hearing our English, the wife said, "Hello," and in exasperation, her accent thickly British, asked, "Well, what do you think of the *French* service?" It was obvious what *she* thought.

Stunned out of our eulogistic rhapsodies, we were a little taken aback, but in light of the food and the service we had experienced *this* evening, we were not unsympathetic.

The youngest of their three children, all boys, smiled sweetly at us, but his brothers (the elder of the two looked to be about eight), seemed tired and irritable, and were demanding their father's full attention.

They had spent the last three weeks motoring from England to the south of France, into Provence, and back up again, the wife explained, seeming grateful to be speaking English. Everywhere, she said, they had found the French to be "less than hospitable."

Complimenting the boys, Mona remarked on the difficulty of travel with children. Since their plan was to spend the night in Savonnieres, I recomended my favorite patisserie and told them about the better, less expensive food being served at the Marina.

When the time came for us to leave, we said good-bye, wishing them well, but still their dinners had not arrived.

"See," I said to Jack outside, "I told you the French are not crazy for the English."

We took a last walk by the river, past the *Saponaria*, and along the campground. There were a few dim lanterns glowing in some of the tents and the flickering light from a television could be seen in one of the trailers, the sound of kids' laughter breaking the darkness.

The British family's tale of unhappy receptions was the complete opposite of what we had experienced this past month. The French might have a reputation for inhospitality, yet, excepting tonight, we had found them considerate and charming. Mona and Lettie discussed the hardships of a three-week motor trip with a trio of boys under the age of eight. I admitted I wouldn't want to attempt it for three hours.

For the last time we climbed the hill of Rue de la Liberté, unlocked the gate, and went in. It was time to settle up the last of the bills and pack for the morning.

Gathering around the table, we added up the final receipts and passed the francs back and forth until everyone had been reimbursed. Thanks to Mona's scrupulous accounting, and the fact that we did most of our own cooking rather than eating in restaurants, the total cost for the month (not including airfares)—*for the house, food, and the car rental*—came to under four hundred dollars a week each.

Saturday, August 15

THE ALARM WAS RINGING when I awoke to Mackie calling to us from downstairs. The coffee was already brewing. We dressed and drank a hasty cupful standing out on the terrace, watching the birds flutter through the branches of the peach tree. Washing up, I dried the cups, put them carefully back into the cabinet, then unplugged and rinsed out the coffeepot while Rory and Jack carried suitcases out to the car. Oddly, I felt as though I were closing up my own house, not unlike the way it had felt leaving Maine to come here.

"Don't forget to write in the book!" Mona reminded us.

On the last page of the green book the owner of the house had requested that the guests write their impressions in the journal of the house, or *livre d'or*—the golden book. There were several of these entries, and reading them over this past month we had found them filled with grateful reports of happy times.

"We came as a group," I wrote, "a gardener, an architect, two art teachers, a pair of lovers, a teenager, and a cook. We toasted you and your husband for creating this truly beautiful and magic place, and sadly, I feel as though I'm leaving a love affair too soon."

≈ ≈ ≈

WHEN IT WAS FINALLY time to go, Jack opened the gates and Mackie pulled the car out onto the street. Lettie was disappointed not to see Monsieur Deek. There was no one to bid us farewell. I climbed into the backseat, watching Mona locking the gates behind us for the last time, and slipping the keys into the mailbox for Marie-Claire. Grumbling, Mona wedged herself in beside Rory, Jack, and me for one final, sardine-packed journey.

"Everybody comfortable?" Mackie asked. We pulled away down the hill of Rue de la Liberté and onto the highway.

I never looked back. Not at the house or the street or Savonnieres. I didn't need to. It would exist inside me for all of my life. It was not just the end of a vacation, a good-bye to a wonderful month, but the beginning of something that I had yet to realize. I fixed my gaze forward as we headed for home.

Epilogue

HOW DO YOU WALK AWAY FROM SOMETHING YOU love, the only thing that has ever brought you success and a steady paycheck? Where do you go next? Our time in Savonnieres had impressed on me the need for a change, but cooking had been the source of my professional accomplishments.

To turn my back on those years in the kitchen would squander the expertise gained by thirty years' experience.

I thought about the times in my life when I had "heated up the pan": moving to New York; my decision to leave New York for Maine; opening the restaurant; and, most recently, our resolve to go to France.

From the first days of our stay at the house, Lettie, Jack, and Mona had kept a journal of our menus on a yellow-lined legal pad, even including in it the labels from the wine we had consumed. Most of my life, no matter what the event—life and death, happiness or sadness—I've been able to recall what was eaten. But as I began to transcribe this diary of dinners, it worked in reverse, the food brought to mind the occasions of the day, and these became the genesis of the preceding pages.

The experience of my visit to Clos-Luce, and in particular da Vinci's dictum on *work*, proved an invaluable reassurance that my *efforts* could make possible the achievement of my goals. On my sixty-second birthday I opted to apply for Social Security (which I prefer to consider an "arts grant") and began to devote myself full-time to writing.

JAMES HALLER is an international award–winning master chef, author, and lecturer. He was the executive chef, founder, and owner of the Blue Strawbery restaurant in Portsmouth, New Hampshire, and the Lee Fontain Carriage House in Memphis, Tennessee. He is currently the owner/operator of James Haller's Kitchen, where he acts as a food consultant and gives classes. Haller is the author of three cookbooks, a food/fitness book, and *What to Eat When You Don't Feel Like Eating*, a book for feeding terminally ill people, which has sold over 500,000 copies.